D0547281

Advance Praise

"Liz's journey is nothing short of inspirational."
—ALEXANDER LUDWIG, ACTOR

"Liz is an inspiring young woman mountaineer, and I loved climbing with her to the top of the world Mount Everest in 2016."
—TENDI SHERPA, TWELVE-TIME EVEREST SUMMITER

"Liz took the Vancouver Canucks flag to the top of Everest and then presented it to me afterwards. Read her gripping story about what she encountered and the personal growth she experienced."
—TREVOR LINDEN, FORMER PRESIDENT AND PLAYER OF THE VANCOUVER CANUCKS

"Through her inspiring book, Liz will share with you how she conquered the highest peaks in the world and how the journey ultimately shaped who she became."
—PETRA NĚMCOVÁ, MODEL, AUTHOR, AND COFOUNDER, ALL HANDS AND HEARTS

Written in the Snow

LIONCREST
PUBLISHING

COPYRIGHT © 2019 ELIZABETH ROSE

All rights reserved.

WRITTEN IN THE SNOW

My Journey to the Seven Summits

ISBN 978-1-5445-1373-7 *Paperback*

978-1-5445-1372-0 *Ebook*

To everyone who believed in me, you got me to the
summit. To everyone who didn't, so did you.

To anyone reading this book, explore the world, believe
in yourself, and cherish those who believe in you.

Contents

Introduction

My heart is racing. I've slipped against the icy rock wall near Everest's majestic summit right at the start of my descent. Moments ago, I was standing on top of the world taking in views of the Himalayas, the bright blue sky contrasting beautifully against the flapping swarm of colorful flags planted by fellow climbers. Suddenly, I found myself swinging in the air, my black and yellow mountaineering boots dangling off the top of the world's highest peak. My crampons—the metal spikes on the bottom of my boots that have given me traction and grounding in the face of some of the most challenging environments on the planet—have sliced my Sherpa's snowsuit. Feathers are flying everywhere.

For a moment, I worry that I have cut not just his snowsuit, but also through to his leg. The weather is about to turn, and we need to make it down to camp. We need to make it down fast.

Thanks to the combination of the rope and belay device, my Sherpa and I catch ourselves. I learn the only thing injured is his very expensive snowsuit. Still, I'm on the verge of a full-fledged panic attack and I begin to cry, making it impossible to catch my breath.

I have to hold my oxygen mask to my face because my tears have soaked through the suction. My glasses are fogged from the moisture.

First, I can't breathe, and then, I can't see. I ask my Sherpa—a Nepalese man with tanned skin, kind eyes, and now, a seriously dysfunctional snowsuit—for a moment to catch my breath and regroup. "There's no time to stop," he says. "Everyone is going up and down along this one rope, and we need to move."

So, I did what I'd continue to do throughout my journey to summit the highest mountain on each continent and, looking back, what I'd done many times over the course of my twenty-five years: I said yes. I trusted myself. I kept going.

* * *

The memory of swinging near the top of Everest is a vivid one in my mind, but I have countless others. The hours before I reached the summit were brutal. But, as I'll cover in detail later in the book, I summited strong. Together with my group, I left Camp Three for the summit push around 10:00 p.m., when it was pitch dark and freezing. Every zipper pull and every exposed part of me—every strand of hair peeking out from my hat—was covered in ice thanks to the -40 C/F weather. When the group was stopped or moving slowly, I stomped my feet and clapped my hands to prevent getting frostbite. My oxygen mask was making my mouth dry, and the sips of water I'd had that day didn't feel like enough. Summiting, though, was worth it all.

After slipping on Everest's peak, the rest of the way down wasn't much better. When I finally pulled myself together from swinging from the highest mountain on the planet, next came passing the dead body that I had seen on my way up, haunting my thoughts the rest of the way. I tried not to look and just stay focused on the summit. Only the vintage of his boots told me he had been there for decades; otherwise his body looked perfectly preserved. He wasn't wearing gloves, and his flesh was exposed and flawlessly frozen. You'd think his body would be covered by snow, but instead, lying on the windy ridge, it was in plain sight atop the snow. In my head, I kept wondering what had gone wrong? Was he on the way up or down? A running list of endless possibilities—it could've been anything. Seeing his body on the way down was a wakeup call that I needed to get off this mountain—as soon as possible.

That first night, we could only get to Camp Three—a slope dotted with the orange and yellow tents of other climbers heading down. I wanted to get past Camp Three because it was still located above 26,000 feet, also known as "the Death Zone." In the Death Zone, your body becomes deprived of oxygen and can start to break down. We didn't have enough daylight to go further, so we camped in our down snowsuits and sleeping bags with oxygen masks over our faces.

The next day, we woke up and continued our descent.

A strong windstorm made the already treacherous path even more dangerous. At one point, we had to face our back toward the wind and walk down the mountain backwards. At another point, we took shelter at Camp Two. Or rather, we *tried* to take shelter in the only two tents that hadn't been blown apart in the storm. We piled into the two remaining tents and attempted to wait out the weather, but eventually it became clear: there was no waiting it out. We needed to keep going.

When we reached Camp One several hours later, most of the climbers in my group wanted to stop to sleep. I understood. I was tired, too. My oxygen bottle felt like lead in my backpack, and I was exhausted. Still, the thought of reaching Advanced Base Camp—reaching a satellite phone to let my parents know I was alive—overtook my body and gave me strength. One other climber and I set off with our Sherpas, leaving the rest of the climbers behind.

When I reached Advanced Base Camp, I was ecstatic. I felt lucky to be there and thrilled to be safe. I couldn't wait to reach out to my parents. They'd found out I had summited via a social media post from someone who worked for the climbing company, but they didn't know I'd made it down in one piece. I was able to call them quickly and I think that was the happiest they've ever been to hear my voice. They were so relieved that I was safely off the mountain.

Later that night, I lay wide awake in my tent, my mind racing, trying to process what I had just accomplished. Reflecting on my experience, I emailed my parents:

> Sorry to put you guys through the pain of waiting to hear from me. I am truly grateful for the accomplishment and the experience, but zero chance my kids are climbing Everest. I wouldn't even want a friend to go. It was truly that insane. The biggest summit is being down in one piece. I only have a few blisters and some sore spots on my face from my oxygen mask, sunglasses, and windburn. I am so lucky to be alive.

My name is Liz Rose, and I am the youngest Canadian—and one of fewer than one hundred women—ever to have climbed the Seven Summits: all in less than three years.

I have always worked hard to achieve my goals, and I was lucky to have an amazing support system. I'm thankful for all the opportunities I've had, but the point of sharing my story and my journey through the Seven Summits is not to promote climbing. Instead, I want to inspire you to find and reach your own goals. You don't need to climb huge mountains to get the same experience and adventure in your life.

In this book, I'll take you on my journey and hopefully motivate you to find your own. To leave you wanting to say 'yes' to more opportunities. To do hard things. To open doors and embrace what's new. To find what you're passionate about and go after it. To stay positive in the face of challenges. To chase big, meaningful goals. And, if you're at a crossroads in your life (like I was), to take action. To find your summit, whatever that looks like.

Here is my story.

Chapter 1

Sea Level

It is possible for ordinary people to choose to be extraordinary.

—ELON MUSK

Climbing the Seven Summits was never on my radar until I found myself adrift and at a crossroads in my life. I had been living in the United States for five years, attending university and film school. After graduation, I hoped to find work in Manhattan. As a Canadian who had attended school in the US, I had a one-year work visa, but at the end of the day, no one wanted to hire a Canadian who could work in America for only a limited amount of time. Finally, I got fed up and decided to move back to Canada, where I could more easily find a job.

Not quite ready to return to my hometown of Vancouver, I moved to Toronto. I was craving someplace new and exciting, somewhere to start the beginning of my next chapter. So in good fashion, I showed up in Toronto with no job and no place to live. I stayed in an Airbnb as I started my job search. My resumé was solid, I was well connected, and I was eager to start working. What could go wrong? I'd have a job in no time, right?

Wrong.

After two months of searching, I still didn't have a job and now I was getting frustrated. I vividly remember sitting up in bed late at night, still at my Airbnb, staring at the glow of the computer screen. Post after post, I clicked "apply" and waited. I constantly refreshed LinkedIn, looking for the right opportunity or the right connection. Nothing worked. I knew I needed to do something to fulfill myself; I felt like I would go crazy if I just kept searching, staring, and surfing. I desperately wanted to accomplish something. I wanted adventure. I wanted forward motion.

So, I began a different kind of search.

KILIMANJARO: THE QUICK FIX

In limbo about what to do next, I considered many options, including taking time off to travel. But I had already done this, having studied abroad in London and experiencing a Semester at Sea. I was very fortunate to be well-travelled early in life.

Exhausted and discouraged with the job search, I started looking online for adventure trips. I stumbled upon a Canadian adventure company that happened to be located down the street from my place in Toronto. Browsing the company's website, an intriguing outdoor adventure caught my eye: "climb Mount Kilimanjaro!" This seemed perfect, especially when I remembered that a friend's mom had done this and thoroughly enjoyed her journey. In addition, I wanted to do something right away, and I wanted to go for about a week; Kilimanjaro trips could be done in six days, and there was one taking off soon. I felt climbing Kilimanjaro would feed that craving in me to accomplish something, feel good about myself, and return to my job search with new motivation.

I was quite confident I could reach the summit of Kilimanjaro because I was in good physical shape, and although I had no intense hiking experience per se, I had a history of being athletic. From the time I was four, I had skis on my feet, and I grew up playing every sport, up through high school and university. To top it all off, I have older twin brothers, and I constantly tried to keep up with them, in sports and on the slopes. Later, during my university days living in Colorado, I spent a lot of time in the mountains. But while I have always been adventurous, I was by no means an accomplished hiker.

A FATHER-DAUGHTER ADVENTURE IS BORN

After I'd found the Kilimanjaro trip, I called my mom and told her about it. "Do you think I have a chance of Dad going with me?" I asked. I would have been happy to go alone, but my dad loves father-daughter activities, and I get my adventurous spirit from him. In the past, we'd gone skydiving together and taken a handful of trips, just the two of us. I thought it was worth a shot.

"Well, you got your dad to jump out of a plane and fly in a glider when he's afraid of heights, so only you could get him to climb Africa's tallest mountain!" my mother replied. "Go for it!"

Before I asked my dad to join me, I did my prep work: I looked at the calendar with my mom and figured out when my dad would be free. The logistics were all taken care of. Then, I made the call.

"You've got to be kidding! Do you know how high that mountain is? And where in Africa is it?" my father asked when I told him about the trip. "Do you think we'll be able to do it?"

"Yeah, we're both fit," I said. "I think we'll be fine."

"Okay, let me think about it," he said.

The next day, my phone rang and I saw it was Dad. As soon as I answered, he said, "Poli, poli! You better know what that means!"

"Slowly, slowly!" I yelled, knowing that *poli* means "slowly" in Swahili. It's a term used often while climbing Kilimanjaro.

It was official: Kilimanjaro was on, and my dad and I were going together.

NEW ADVENTURES ABOUND

The day after Dad and I had booked our flights to Tanzania, I got a job offer. My dad was happy for me but also concerned because we'd just booked our flights for the soon-approaching trip. I told him not to worry because the hiring process would likely be long, and everything would work out. It wasn't my Toronto dream job, but it was still exciting: I would be filming a TV show on a cruise ship while traveling the world.

The trip to Kilimanjaro was the start of a new journey for me in many ways. The climb initiated my drive to climbing the Seven Summits and became the gateway to so many lessons I'd learn along the way.

Chapter 2

19,341 ft. (5,895 m) above Sea Level

You have to leave the city of your comfort zone and go into the wilderness of your intuition.

—ALAN ALDA

When I decided to climb Mount Kilimanjaro, I knew it was the tallest mountain in Africa, but that was about all I knew. The plan was to summit Kilimanjaro, my dad by my side, and gain a sense of satisfaction and accomplishment. Then, I'd move on to my new job, and everything else that lay ahead. I sure had no intention of climbing other mountains after that. Clearly, I was wrong.

Kilimanjaro changed everything for me.

PREPARATION

Two weeks before our climb, I moved from Toronto to Vancouver. My dad and I didn't even own hiking boots. We were both physically fit, so we weren't too worried about the training, but the company taking us was. When I went into the office to sign up, they expressed concern, telling me it was a hard hike for which people train extensively. My friend also informed me her mom had trained for about a year before she made the climb, and she mentioned it wasn't exactly something you just sign up for at the last minute...*Oops!* Still, my dad and I are optimistic people, and we tried not to let those concerns get to us.

We were worried about one thing, though: getting the necessary gear and breaking in our boots ahead of time to avoid getting blisters. Another friend of ours had recently climbed Kilimanjaro and gave us a fantastic packing list.

After we bought the things we needed—hiking pants, merino wool base layer tops and bottoms, hiking socks, boots, and so on—we went on a few local hikes to break in our boots. That was the extent of our training. The local hikes we did in Vancouver were on wide-open trails that weren't steep. At one point my dad asked, "Do you think it's going be like this?"

"No, not really," I admitted. "I think it's going to be a lot harder."

We had no idea what we were getting ourselves into.

THE MOUNTAIN AND THE GROUP

Mount Kilimanjaro is the world's largest freestanding mountain, meaning that it's not part of a mountain range—it stands alone. The fourth highest of the Seven Summits, it's nicknamed 'Kili.'

Our journey began in late December, and Dad and I flew nine hours from Vancouver to Amsterdam. We spent a few days there adjusting to the time difference, sightseeing, and celebrating New Year's before taking the eight-hour flight to Moshi, Tanzania. When we landed in Moshi, we met our group of five other climbers: two young women from the United Kingdom who were best friends, an older couple from Australia, and a young man from the United Kingdom. Discreetly checking them out, I noticed the two girls had an adventurous spirit, but they didn't look like seasoned hikers. They were warm, upbeat, and excited to be on the climb together. In contrast, the older Aussie couple seemed to bicker with each other from the moment we met them at the orientation dinner. The solo young man from the UK was energetic, very talkative, and thrilled to be on a reading break from Oxford's law school. We'll call him "Oxford" from now on.

We also had three guides, twenty-one porters who carried food, tents, sleeping bags, and so on, and one chef.

Before we started the climb, my dad and I talked about what would happen if either he or I couldn't finish. This was an important conversation to have and we didn't want to leave it to the heat of the moment. We agreed that if one of us couldn't continue for whatever reason, we wanted the other person to summit, regardless. Of course, we wanted to stick together, but we also didn't want to hold each other back from the opportunity of standing on top of the roof of Africa.

THE ASCENT

There are several routes up Kilimanjaro. We hiked the Rongai Route, which started near the Kenya border and is one of the least traveled routes up the mountain. The thought of less crowded trails was very appealing. The trail goes up one side of Kilimanjaro and then down a direct traditional route on the other side.

The trip dates for this route worked with our timeline and my dad's work schedule, so—without knowing much about any of the routes—we went with it.

The Rongai Route started in a lush forest, engulfing us in a tropical green canopy. It was *hot*; about 28°C. I wore lightweight trekking pants and a black T-shirt, with my hair pulled back into two long braids, and a red bandana tied around my head. Of course, this outfit was very pre-planned, as I knew there would be lots of father-daughter photos to be taken. With my GoPro camera in hand and my pack on my back, I was ready for the adventure. Everyone was excited to get started, and the energy in our group was high. Most of the time, we hiked single-file up the winding trail for about four to six hours per day. Summit day, however, was much longer because of the distance and higher altitude.

The chef cooked a hot breakfast and dinner every day. Most dinners consisted of hearty vegetable soups, stews, or pasta—easy to prepare and great for sharing. During the day, we ate snacks as we continued up the mountain. The porters carried our gear and set up our campsite before we arrived with our guides. The porters were young, fit males that did more than carry—they took the time to get to know us. They also put on a memorable singing and dancing show with traditional music for us, allowing us to see a piece of their culture during our precious time on the mountain.

At the end of each day, we were exhausted. My dad and I weren't used to hiking the distances required. Every night, we were so excited to simply lie down in our tent. One night, we climbed in before dinner to rest and were too tired to take our boots off because we knew we'd just have to put them right back on for dinner. We fell asleep with our feet out the door of the tent—boots on and all—just to conserve that bit of energy.

As the altitude increased, the temperature dropped. We experienced a few hailstorms, both while sleeping and while hiking. Whenever it snowed or hailed on the trail, our lead guide would pull out a massive umbrella and keep on hiking. It was a funny sight. He made the climb seem like a routine walk in the park. The scenery also changed as we got higher up the mountain and traveled through three completely different climate zones. We started out in the rainforest, moved through the low alpine, and ended in the high alpine zone. The wildlife and vegetation became sparser and sparser the higher we got, and with each change, we felt almost as if we had exited and entered new worlds.

One of the biggest challenges on Kili was dealing with the altitude. It is a very high mountain to summit in such a short amount of time. Our guides were cautious; every night, they monitored everyone's oxygen saturation levels by placing a device on our fingertips. This reading indicated how our bodies were adjusting to the altitude.

This was our first experience with high-altitude hiking, and the first day, my dad didn't feel well. Not surprisingly, he also worried about how he would feel in the days to come, as we continued to climb higher. Dad and I both took Diamox, a drug that helps the body deal with altitude change. Thankfully, after a few hours, his headache began to dissipate and he started to feel more like himself.

To help with altitude adjustment, the guides made sure we moved slowly and drank an overabundance of water. Every few minutes, they would say in Swahili, "poli, poli." If you move too quickly, you are more susceptible to altitude sickness, which feels like a bad hangover: nausea and a headache. The only time I experienced altitude sickness was on summit day.

Although my dad and I were dead tired at the end of each day, we treasured the whole experience. We remained positive and felt lucky to be going through the journey together. Each morning, we were ready to start hiking and to see what that day had to offer. We loved the idea of reaching the top, and every day brought us closer to that goal. On certain days, we could see Kili ahead of us on the trail, a picture-perfect view just like you would see on a postcard. We were so excited to get to stand on top of such an iconic mountain.

THE SUMMIT

Summit day—January 7, 2015—began at midnight. The day before, we'd hiked to a certain point, had dinner, and then rested until midnight when the guides woke us up to get ready. It had snowed while we were in our tents, so there was ankle-deep powder surrounding our camp. It was pitch black and bitterly cold, so we piled on warm clothes and put on our headlamps.

The first part of Kili's summit climb is very steep, and we traversed it in a zig-zag pattern—walking a long way to one side and then back the other way—rather than hike straight up. Normally this section takes people five hours to climb, but it took us longer because of all the snow. Our only source of light was from our headlamps, which meant we had no idea how much farther we had to climb. It felt like a never-ending hill.

We reached the top of Gilman's Point just as the sun was rising. We were exhausted, and at this point, my head was throbbing. To try and make me feel better, Oxford gave my dad and me a British candy called Percy's Pigs—a pink gummy candy that burst with fruity flavor. In the moment, it was the best-tasting thing I had ever eaten. It gave me the energy boost I needed to continue. Although technically we were on top of the mountain at this point, we still had to hike another couple of hours to reach the sign that says, "Congratulations, you've reached the top of Kilimanjaro." Nevertheless, we were thrilled because it was finally daylight, the view was gorgeous, and the steepest part was over. At this point, our group had dwindled to my dad, myself, and Oxford. The Australian couple had decided to turn back and give up on the summit, and the other two girls were behind us.

We finally reached the sign on the flat, wide top of the mountain—the biggest summit space of all the Seven

Summits. I took off my gloves to take pictures and my hands went completely numb—for a split second, I had forgotten that it was still utterly freezing outside. We managed to do a photo shoot, but it was quick. I hugged my dad at the top of Kilimanjaro. We were so overjoyed to have finally reached the top together.

We started down the other side of the mountain to descend to our next camp. By the time we reached it, we had been awake for sixteen hours and were absolutely exhausted—so exhausted that we decided to skip dinner and stay in our sleeping bags. We had eaten soup almost every meal, and the last thing we wanted at that point was more soup. Instead, we ate beef jerky and mint-chocolate Clif Bars. It was an awful combination, but it tasted amazing in the comfort of our sleeping bags. The chef and our guides were not happy that we skipped dinner because they were worried that we were sick, but we reassured them we had snacks of our own and needed the extra rest.

Hiking back down Kilimanjaro the following day, we took a much more direct route. We made it all the way down in one day. The lower we got, the warmer it became, and soon we were wearing T-shirts again. Our group celebrated at the bottom with Kilimanjaro beers and tried to soak in our accomplishment of the past six days.

Summiting Kilimanjaro with my dad was one of the most special events of my then-twenty-four years. Despite the fact that neither of us were big hikers, we made it to the summit without any major trouble. It was a monumental accomplishment for both of us—and an extraordinary one because of the fact that we did it together. To this day, we reference our time on that climb; it's something that will live with us forever.

Hiking Kili taught me several practical lessons about climbing. I learned to drink lots of water, as it both prevents and cures mild altitude sickness. I also learned to move slowly, as altitude hiking is all about pacing yourself. You may think you can go faster, but to help your body acclimatize, listening to your guides is of the utmost importance. Last but certainly not least, I learned to wear sunscreen. On summit day, we left in the dark, and none of us put on sunscreen. By the time the sun came out and we were at 19,000 feet, we weren't thinking clearly. Sunscreen was the last thing on our minds. The entire hike down, the sun was reflecting directly off the snow and onto my face, and I was left with third-degree burns.

Never. Again.

TRY NEW THINGS

My dad and I had never done anything remotely like the Kilimanjaro hike, and the accomplishment brought us so much joy. You never know where a new activity is going to lead, or what you're going to like doing until you try it. It's important to have new experiences—to put yourself out there, even if it scares you. Take risks and test your body in new environments. You never know; you may find new passions and interests that lead to so many other opportunities. While hiking Kili, I fell in love with the idea of going on treks and adventures, and summiting mountains. Saying yes to this opportunity opened the door to so many more that would continue to shape my world for the better.

Chapter 3

17,598 ft. (5,364 m) above Sea Level

Setting goals is the first step in turning the invisible into visible.

—TONY ROBBINS

Directly after I returned from hiking Kili, I began my new job filming a daily television talk show on a cruise ship for six months at a time. I also used a GoPro to film shore excursions such as snorkeling or cave explorations. In a lot of ways, it was the ideal job because I got to travel, explore, and film all at the same time—and was paid for it.

After working for six months, I had two months off. I wanted to do something exciting, partly because I was scheduled to have a follow-up surgical operation in the coming months, and I would be inactive for weeks. I wasn't too worried about the surgery, but it was still a significant two-day procedure. I have grown up getting surgeries on a vascular anomaly over my forehead and eye, and though I had been through it before, I wanted to have another exciting adventure just in case something went wrong on the operating table.

When I was looking for my pre-surgery adventure, I noticed on social media that a friend had recently traveled to Everest Base Camp. From the looks of her photos, the trip looked *incredible*. Instantly, I decided that hiking to the base of Everest was exactly what I wanted to do.

Originally, I had asked my dad if he would come with me because our Kili experience had gone so well. He said he'd like to go, but, because it was so last minute, he couldn't make it work with his schedule. So, I signed up to go alone.

The next day, though, my mom got wind of my plans and posed a valid question. "Why didn't anyone ask if I wanted to go?"

My dad and I looked at each other.

"Okay!" we said in unison. "You're in!"

"Well, I didn't say I wanted to," she said. "I was just wondering if you were going to ask me."

"No," we said. "Now you're going."

My mom is very active and athletic, but, like my dad, hiking isn't something she had much experience in. It also should be noted that my mom is legally blind, so I was especially proud of her for accepting this challenge. Just as Dad and I had no gear when we signed up for Kili, Mom didn't own any gear either, and we had only a few weeks to prepare for our mother-daughter adventure.

Hiking to Everest Base Camp is a classic fifteen-day trek in Nepal. Many people do it for the sole reason that it's a gorgeous trek and a great way to immerse themselves in the local culture and community. In addition, hikers have the opportunity to see where people who climb Everest live for two months of their climbing expedition.

Most hikers who complete the Everest Base Camp trek have no intention of ever climbing to the summit. They just want to experience the Himalayas and get a sense of what Everest is all about. I was not one of these people, but I just didn't know it yet.

JOURNEY TO BASE CAMP

I left the cruise ship and returned to Canada a couple of weeks before the trip to Everest Base Camp. My mom needed to buy her gear, and we both needed to start training. We went on a couple hikes together to prep for our journey. I figured it would be easier than climbing Kili, so I wasn't too worried. We flew from Vancouver to Dubai to soak up the sun for a few days before our trek. I went for a sunrise wakeboard, an activity I try to do in every city I visit that is near the water, before boarding our early morning flight to Kathmandu. Going from Dubai to Kathmandu was quite the change in culture. We spent one night in the heart of the bustling city of Kathmandu before carrying on to Lukla, where our hike would begin. We made our way through the chaotic Kathmandu airport and boarded the tiny, sketchy-looking plane that would take us the rest of the way to Lukla. Lukla is notorious for having one of the most dangerous runways in the world. I lucked out with a window seat and enjoyed the breathtaking views of the epic snow-covered peaks. The runway at Lukla isn't flat; rather it's on a very steep hill. I have no fear of flying, so I found the landing exciting, but some people were definitely on edge and completely out of their comfort zone. Mom squeezed my hand in fear as I excitedly filmed the landing through the window with my GoPro.

Our climbing group was larger than I had anticipated: an Australian girl, a South African girl, a Canadian couple on their honeymoon, a man from Austria, a woman from Denmark, three other Canadians, me, and my mom. All of our group members were in their twenties, with the exception of my mom, who was fifty-seven. Our eight-day hike to Everest Base Camp started as soon as we got off the plane in Lukla, and we passed through several small mountain towns over the course of the journey. Surrounded by the Himalayas, we crossed over rickety suspension bridges swaying high above coursing rivers below. The scenery on the trek was absolutely gorgeous. We were constantly passed by yaks on the trail carrying gear to Base Camp, and moved aside to let them go ahead. Colorful prayer flags—signifying good luck and blessed by monks living throughout the surrounding mountain villages—were all over the place: strung across the trees, bridges, and anything else you could possibly tie a flag to. Everywhere we looked, the views were beyond breathtaking, and I couldn't help to think I would want to bring my kids back here one day. There were only three times we could see Everest itself as we hiked, because of where the route to Base Camp is positioned, and even then, we could only see the very tip of it.

Although some sections of the trek were fairly steep, the overall hike wasn't extremely strenuous. Still, the days were quite long and we could definitely feel the altitude. At night, we stayed in teahouses owned by local families who cooked for us and gave us our own rooms and beds to sleep in. We sat by the fire with entire host families, children and all, reflecting and connecting in whatever ways we could.

Namche Bazaar, a town we stayed in for a couple of nights for acclimatization during our trek, is a mountain village on the route to Everest Base Camp. It is a gorgeous, vibrant little village nestled within the Himalayan peaks about halfway to Base Camp, complete with bakeries, gear shops, and spas galore (offering massages that I would have loved to get). It was so much fun to see the local children running around playing. Kids are kids, no matter where in the world you are.

When we finally reached Base Camp, we stayed for thirty to forty-five minutes to explore and take pictures by a pile of prayer flags and a poster board that read: "Everest Base Camp 5364m," which had been placed by fellow trekkers. Unlike Kili, there was no permanent, famous sign. From April to June, during Everest climbing season, Base Camp is a tent city melting pot of people of different nationalities all awaiting the opportunity to summit Everest. We were there five months before climbing season, though, so camp was just a large, uneven rocky area laden with prayer flags. After we all had our photos taken and had celebrated with "Everest" beers—a brand you find in Nepal—we made our way back down.

FINDING MY PASSION

At the beginning of the trip to Everest Base Camp, I became friends with a doctor from South Africa. It turned out we had been born on the exact same day and year! She told me all about her aunt who had climbed Everest and all Seven Summits. This was the first time I'd ever heard the concept of climbing the highest peak on each of the seven continents; little did I know that hearing this would change my life. After that conversation, we arrived at our first teahouse, and I paid five dollars for Wi-Fi so I could google Seven Summits and learn more about what it all meant. Knowing I wouldn't have Wi-Fi for long, I took a screen shot of what I'd found and saved it to my phone for future reference.

As I reviewed the list of the Seven Summits and their elevations, I realized I had already climbed one: Kilimanjaro. Being at Base Camp made me obsess about Everest and the other mountains, and I made the decision right then and there that I was going to climb them all. I showed my mom the list and told her my intention, and we discussed it for the rest of the trip. At that point, climbing the Seven Summits was simply a lifelong goal— something I knew I wanted to achieve and "someday" would. I didn't know then that someday would come far sooner than I thought.

During the trek to Everest Base Camp, I set my intentions: I wanted to pursue mountaineering. The incredible scenery, the beautiful mountains, the Nepalese culture full of kind, giving, and welcoming people—all of it made me want to come back and keep climbing.

In some ways, my experience hiking to Everest Base

Camp—although it wasn't even close to the most difficult hike I'd done or would do—was a turning point in my life.

SET GOALS, EVEN IF THEY FEEL BIG

Mount Everest was invisible for most of the trip to Base Camp, but I could feel it in the distance. I had found my passion and set a goal to climb the Seven Summits. Because I kept moving forward, my goal became increasingly visible in my mind—even if Everest wasn't. Once you discover what you want to do, make a plan and keep pushing forward. Sometimes it can feel like trudging through quicksand uphill but keep going.

LEARN ABOUT AND EXPERIENCE NEW CULTURES

At the teahouses I stayed at on my way to Everest Base Camp, I fell in love with the Nepalese culture. Sitting around fires with families, feeling their warmth, and sharing their relaxed energy opened my eyes to a world I had never experienced. As you set out on your own journey—whatever that may be—remember to keep your eyes and heart open to the people you meet along the way. Meeting new people and embracing new cultures can expand your life in immeasurable ways.

Chapter 4

22,841 ft. (6,962 m) above Sea Level

There are no regrets
in life, just lessons.

—JENNIFER ANISTON

After our Everest Base Camp climb, I had my scheduled surgery. It had seemed to go well, but shortly after the operation, when I was supposed to report to the cruise ship for my next rotation, my doctors said they needed me back in New York for a second surgery. As a result, I had to bow out of my contract on the cruise ship. It was a legitimate medical reason, so I wasn't fired but I was, however, "out of rotation"—an unfortunate situation that meant I had no idea when I would get my next contract. They could call at any time; I could be waiting two weeks or five months.

It was February of 2016 and I was back in Vancouver recovering from the second surgery. I quickly fell into a rut filled with frustration and boredom. I was anxious to get back to work or to just pursue *something*, but I felt stuck. In an effort to try and help pull me out, my dad suggested I research another mountain to help pass the time during the work gap. Again, I pulled up the screenshot of the Seven Summits I'd saved from my trip to Everest Base Camp. I researched which peak was in climbing season, and there was only one: Aconcagua in Argentina. Although Aconcagua is the second highest of the Seven Summits, it's not a very technical climb, so I was hopeful a mountaineering company would let me on the trip. The last available departure date for any company given was February 21, because it was the end of the climbing season for Aconcagua, so I had to act fast.

PREPARATION

On a Monday, I called the mountaineering company to inquire if there was still room on their final ascent of the season. After asking about my experience and assuring me there were enough guides to help me learn the necessary skills on the spot, they agreed to take me. I flew out that Friday.

The intervening four days were hectic because I had to purchase all new gear. While I had supplies from my previous ventures, Aconcagua was different—this was a mountaineering trip that involved climbing over ice and snow. My hiking boots and clothes for walking up trails were fine for Everest Base Camp and Kili, but I needed special gear for Aconcagua: double-layered mountaineering boots, crampons, an ice axe, a climbing harness, a very warm sleeping bag, and a massive down-filled parka.

I didn't want to ask the doctors who had performed my recent surgery whether I was cleared to go climb, one reason being that I still had the remnants of dissolvable stitches in my face. But just as when my dad and I had set off to hike Kili with minimal training, I wasn't worried. I was hyper-aware, however, that because I had been recovering from my surgeries, I hadn't exercised since the Everest Base Camp hike nearly four months earlier. Still, I felt physically fine and had always been fit, so I didn't think climbing Aconcagua would come down to my current level of fitness. If I couldn't make it, I reasoned, it would be due to the weather or altitude sickness.

My parents were traveling when I signed up for the Aconcagua trip. Talking to my dad about the climb and buying the gear, I remember he said something that stuck with me: "Honestly, this will be the test of whether you like mountain climbing. I feel like you'll know whether this is your passion, or not."

He was right. Aconcagua would be the trip that would prove to me I loved mountain climbing—I just didn't know it yet.

THE MOUNTAIN AND THE GROUP

New gear in hand, I left Canada and flew into Mendoza, Argentina. My guide met me at the airport and took me to the hotel to meet the rest of the group. The next morning, we drove a few hours to reach the actual provincial park gate.

My group consisted of two female Australian doctors in their fifties, a man who was about forty, and a woman from Colorado who was my tentmate. After I told her that I had attended the University of Denver, she and I immediately bonded. As soon as the two doctors saw me, though, they seemed concerned. They could tell by the look of my eye that I was fresh out of surgery and asked, "Are you allowed to be here?" I played it off and said, "Yeah, of course."

At dinner that night, the doctors told the guides, "I think we should all get out a piece of paper and write down everyone we think is going to make it to the summit." My tentmate and I looked at each other and said, "Are you kidding me?" The doctors ended up growing on us in the end, but they didn't make the best first impression.

The man in our group had climbed Kili and wanted to do the Seven Summits. To get his body acclimatized to high altitude, he had moved to Leadville, Colorado, the city with the highest elevation in the United States. He was passionate and prepared, but he had come to Aconcagua with a bad ankle injury that would end up slowing him down.

What would hinder all of us in the end was the weather. When you climb Aconcagua, you sign up for a twenty-one-day trip, which includes contingency days to summit in case of inclement weather. There's good reason for that: Aconcagua is notorious for its bad weather. Usually, there's a fifty-fifty shot at having the opportunity for a summit day, but sometimes the weather stands in the way of even trying.

As for the dangers of Aconcagua, they truly are no joke;

climbers have died attempting to summit the mountain. It's not common, but it's also not uncommon. Because of Aconcagua's high altitude, there are doctors at many of the camps who check on climbers during their journeys. In worst-case scenarios, helicopters are available if someone needs rescuing.

THE ASCENT

For the first few days of the trip, hiking Aconcagua wasn't much different from Kili or Everest Base Camp. However, because of the high altitude, the guides had us hike to a certain point and then come back down to sleep at a lower elevation—a process that helps the body acclimatize. It was a new process for me, and it didn't start out well.

On the first day, we arrived at Camp Confluencia and learned how to set up the tents. Shortly thereafter, I began to feel downright awful. We were instructed not to take Diamox until we needed it, so I was hoping I was suffering from a simple migraine that I was prone to getting and wasn't becoming sick from the altitude. We were still only at 11,000 feet—not that high (relatively)—so the fact that I was sick looked bad, especially to the already-critical doctors in my group. I sat in the shade to try to cool off because I had been overheated for hours. My tentmate asked if I was alright, and I immediately broke into tears. The last thing I wanted was for people in my group to know that I was sick or crying, but at that point I couldn't help it—I was overwhelmed with emotion. Physical and mental strain isn't always reserved for the arduous parts of the climb—when you begin to feel your body not cooperate with you right out of the gate, you can't help but begin to feel defeated in all aspects.

My guide took me to the mess tent and measured my heart rate and oxygen levels, which thankfully showed no sign of altitude sickness. Five minutes later, however, I started violently throwing up. I vomited at least six times in those twenty minutes and was left with tear-filled eyes and a pounding headache. I knew I needed to force my body to relax and recover in hopes of a better tomorrow, so I took a migraine pill and lay in the mess tent with my eyes covered by the sleeve of my jacket.

A little while later, the group came in for dinner. I sat up in my chair at the table, but I still wasn't feeling great. I couldn't speak or eat the carrot soup, but I drank some water, and when the main course came, I was able to stomach three potatoes. Soon after, I felt like a whole new person. I had a smile on my face and felt like I was back in the game. In that moment, I'm sure the rest of the group was thinking I was pathetic and had no chance at making it to the top, but a few people who could empathize with how debilitating migraines can be believed a severe headache—not the altitude—had made me sick.

The next day we trekked to Plaza de Mulas, which would become our Base Camp for the climb. Normally, Plaza de Mulas is a bustling Base Camp, swarming with climbers from all over the world beginning their journey for the summit, but because our group had come so late in the season, camp was empty. Here, we rested and sorted our climbing gear for the higher camps.

We went up to Camp One and came straight back down to help our bodies adjust to the higher elevation. After another rest day, we made the full move to Camp One.

Sleeping there did not go so well. I woke up with a terrible headache and ended up vomiting; this time, my guides confirmed altitude sickness. I finally got the okay from my guide to start taking Diamox. In contrast to those at Kili and Everest Base Camp, these guides were strict on this climb about taking Diamox. On future mountains, I knew it was best for me to take it from the start. After I had it in my system, I had to quickly pull myself together to do an acclimatization hike to Camp Two. Breathing in the fresh air on the hike made me feel much better. Camp Two was extremely windy; from that point on, we were all worried about the weather forecast. The guides received reports on the radio, and it was not looking favorable for the next few days. We were able to tough out the wind, and made it to High Camp, where we hoped to summit from. The views from High Camp were beautiful; I was surrounded by stunning snow-covered peaks as far as the eye could see. The journey from Base Camp to High Camp was steep, and the days were long; still, we were just hiking, not climbing. We had not yet used any technical climbing equipment. Our ice axes, helmets, and crampons were for summit day. At this point in the trip, we only had one possible day left to try and summit.

One aspect of the climb I had a hard time adjusting to was using the bathroom. Since Aconcagua is in a Provincial Park, the rules about waste are very strict. To poop, we used a plastic bag attached to a toilet seat that was affixed to a walker. No peeing was allowed in the bag. If we did, the porters would not carry the bag out of camp. The trick was to pee first near some rocks and then make your way to the walker. It took me a while to get used to the process, but soon, I had it down.

Going to the bathroom during the night was also a unique experience. The other women in my group used a pee funnel and a wide-mouth bottle to relieve themselves in the comforts of the tent at night. I'm lucky my twenty-four-year-old bladder didn't require me to relieve myself in the middle of the night because, more often than not, it was freezing and incredibly windy. Some nights the wind was so loud thrashing against our nylon tent walls that it was impossible to sleep.

THE SUMMIT

We woke around 4:00 a.m. on summit day and left an hour later. We started off as a group except for one of the doctors, who decided against trying to summit due to nerves. The only man in our group started the summit attempt with us and then turned back a few hours into it because he was in too much pain from his ankle injury. That left one of the doctors, my tentmate, and me. A little farther on, the guide told the doctor she had to turn back because she was moving too slowly. In the end, my tentmate and I, plus our guide, were the only ones left.

The weather turned very windy, and it was obvious a storm was moving in quickly. Our guide was listening to reports via his black handheld radio. We anxiously awaited his updates as we desperately wanted to summit. Soon it started to snow, and visibility diminished as the clouds rolled in. In my mind, it didn't seem unbearable, but I am not a mountain guide, nor a meteorologist. It didn't matter what I thought.

"Look, I'm getting a weather report and it's not good," our guide told us. "We're going to see how the weather is for the next hour, and then we're going to turn back. No excuses. That's just the way it is."

We continued for another hour, and I still held out hope. Then, our guide told us there was a cave just under 1,000 feet from the summit—a resting spot before people make the final climb. He told us we could go to the cave and then turn back. *Perfect*, I thought. *As long as we're continuing to go up, we might still have a chance.* But as soon as we made it to the cave, he confirmed we had to turn back. While we knew this news was coming, it was still hard to take—turning around so close to the top was excruciatingly disappointing. Still, we knew we could be in danger if we didn't listen; we had to trust the guides and not argue.

As we made the climb back to Base Camp, I was frustrated. But I was not as heartbroken as I'd thought I would be. I was satisfied with the fact that my failure to summit didn't come down to my skills or abilities. The weather was completely out of my control. As far as safety was concerned, I knew that we'd made a smart decision.

Still, I wasn't ready to give up. As we were sitting around a table at Base Camp, the trip manager asked each of us how many hotel nights we would need in Mendoza. He was trying to plan the remainder of our trip. When it was my turn, I answered his question with one of my own.

"Is there any way I can go back up?" I asked.

"Everyone's left Base Camp," he said. "It's the end of the season. That was the last trip."

"Okay, but is it *possible*?" I pressed. "I just want to know if anyone could take me."

"We'll make some phone calls," he said.

Ultimately, the manager said the company could fly a guide in for me if that's what I wanted. I did, but it wasn't a light decision.

I borrowed a computer at Base Camp and messaged my dad for his thoughts. I wrote a long message explaining the situation, not knowing if he would even get the message because of the time difference. Luckily, he responded immediately.

"Okay, go for it, XOXO," he wrote. "But listen to the weather."

"You were supposed to say, 'Come home,'" I wrote. "And 'You gave it such a good shot. You can do it next year.'"

"Oh," Dad replied. "I thought you wanted encouragement."

"Well, I have really mixed feelings," I admitted.

After some more back and forth, I decided to muster up the courage and go for it. At this point, I hadn't showered in two and a half weeks, and there was a snowstorm in Base Camp, so it was freezing. Part of me wanted to shower and go on a wine tour in Mendoza, but I knew in my gut I really yearned to give it all that I had. I decided to go back up instead.

In the end, the company didn't fly in a guide like they'd said; instead, they sent me a teenaged porter who had helped carry our gear on the first attempt. To make the situation more challenging, the porter spoke only Spanish, and I knew only a few words. Needless to say, communication was a struggle.

Before my porter and I began the climb, I said goodbye to the guide I had just spent eighteen days with. I had to choke back tears, feeling highly emotional because I was being handed off to someone I didn't know. Still, I felt okay about the climb itself because I knew the mountain and I knew what I was in for. We set off.

By that time, my body was already acclimatized to the altitude, and the weather forecast for my second attempt was fifty-fifty. Although it didn't call for pure sunshine, I was hopeful for a chance to summit. I spent one night at Aconcagua Base Camp and then went straight to Camp Two.

Camp Two had dome-shaped communal tents for anyone to cook in and use. When I arrived, there were three men in the tent: an Argentinian movie star (we'll just call him Star for short), his photographer, and his guide. My teenaged porter and I joined them, and we formed a group of five for the rest of the climb. The shaggy-blonde-haired movie star, who looked to be in his forties, spoke English well, so he and I became buddies.

The next day, we all climbed to Camp Three and geared up for the final ascent. My second summit day was absolutely perfect—the most beautiful conditions our group could have asked for. We all summited together wearing

T-shirts, had a photo shoot at the top, and then climbed back down to Base Camp.

The hike from Base Camp to the park gates is usually a ten-hour walk, but my new friend had hired a helicopter.

"Liz, we'll leave our bags," Star said. "They can go on the

mules, and we'll take you instead of the luggage. That way you don't have to walk out." It had been a long day, and I accepted the offer—and my first ever ride in a helicopter.

Right outside the park gates is a little town called Los Penitentes; from there, Mendoza is a few more hours' drive. Star and his crew insisted on stopping in Los Penitentes to shower, and I couldn't understand why.

"Can't you just wait until we're in a hotel in a couple hours?" I asked.

"No," he said. "You don't understand. I need a shower. The public doesn't know that I just climbed a mountain. The tabloids will print stories tomorrow saying I don't shower, so we need to stop here." That was the first time I truly understood how famous he actually was.

While they all took turns showering, I sat at a table having coffee. Then, Star joined me.

"So, when are you planning Everest?" he said.

"I don't know," I replied. "Maybe ten years from now."

He said he'd climbed Aconcagua as altitude training for Everest. We'd discussed my job in the film industry, and he explained he was having a videographer go to Everest with him. "Hey, if you're not doing anything next month," he said, "you can come with me. You're a good climber, and you can use my videographer to do any projects you want to do in our Everest group."

"Okay!" I said. "I'm in!"

"What, really?" He said. "You sound like I just asked you for a beer."

"Yeah," I said. "I'll see you in three weeks." Realistically, I knew I had to go home and talk to my family about whether I was a lunatic for even considering climbing the highest mountain in the world in less than a month but being handed an Everest invitation was too rare an opportunity for me to pass up—so I took it.

Arriving back in Mendoza, I hopped out of the car to check in to my hotel. Star got out of the car to hug me goodbye. "See you in Kathmandu!" I said. The second I turned my back to him, a crowd of people ran up calling his name and started taking pictures with their phones. Again, it clicked that he was actually *very* famous. I think he liked me because I knew nothing about him and just treated him like anyone else.

My experience at Aconcagua was far from seamless, but that didn't make it any less impactful. In fact, I learned more from Aconcagua than I had from my other two climbing experiences combined.

ACCEPT THINGS BEYOND YOUR CONTROL

There was nothing I could do about the weather that had prevented me from summiting. Not summiting on the first try had nothing to do with my abilities. I was surprised at my reaction; I thought I would be more upset. I was disappointed, and I allowed myself to feel that way. Even in that tough spot, though, I tried to find a way to give myself another chance. If the weather had been bad on my second attempt, it would have been bad luck, but I still would have known I'd done everything I could. In everything you do—in everything you try to summit in life—safety has to be the priority.

SPEAK UP AND EMBRACE OPPORTUNITY

After we turned back on the first attempt, I stood up for myself and asked for what I wanted: another chance to summit. You never know until you ask, so it's important to verbalize what you want and go after it. If I hadn't taken that chance and stood strong, I wouldn't have met my movie star friend and been presented with the opportunity of a lifetime: climbing Everest.

Chapter 5

29,029 ft. (8,848 m) above Sea Level

If you are offered a seat on a rocket ship, don't ask what seat. Just get on.

—SHERYL SANDBERG

Before I arrived home from Aconcagua, I'd talked to my parents about the invitation to climb Everest. I knew I needed to go home and come back down to Earth before I made a decision, though, because I was on such a high from summiting in Argentina. We talked at length as a family. Putting aside the wave of endorphins I was riding from Aconcagua, my parents and I needed to acknowledge how real and how dangerous attempting Mount Everest can be, or the rest of the Seven Summits for that matter. Mountaineering comes with risks—countless risks that can be boiled down to life or death. I knew that this decision was going to affect many people in my life, and I couldn't selfishly let my youthful, fearless nature be the only deciding voice. My parents and I discussed the worst-case scenarios—what would happen in the event of tragedy. Though I didn't know until "several mountains" later, my parents had a discussion amongst themselves deciding that if they were to offer me their blessing to climb, and something were to happen, they wouldn't let it end their marriage. My parents raised me to not just live, but to be *alive*, not letting fear of the unknown dictate my path. In our conversation, we ultimately agreed that if I were bound to climb Mount Everest someday, this seemed like an ideal opportunity.

I understood that many climbers train for years to climb Everest. I also knew several (often critical) factors would be completely out of my control: the weather might not be good enough to summit or climb at all that season, or I could get altitude sickness. The running list of other unknowns was endless. Still, my parents were supportive, despite feeling nervous and fearing their friends would conclude they were the worst parents in the world for letting me go. I had anxiety about perception, too: I knew I would be judged because I was not a sufficiently experienced mountain climber.

In the end, we ignored what other people might say, and I went for it. I reminded myself that if you live your life constantly worrying about what other people think, you won't get very far.

Having been given the head Sherpa's information, I contacted him. Just because I had been offered the opportunity to join the group did not mean I had been approved to join yet. The Sherpa asked for my climbing resume— that is, all my climbing experience. I didn't have much, but I wrote it up and sent it to him. He liked the fact that I had just come from Aconcagua and that I had climbed it twice. This was a solid test as to how my body functions in high altitude. After I discussed my qualifications with the Sherpa, he gave me the green light. This was it—Everest was happening.

PREPARATION

Once I'd joined the expedition, I had three weeks to prepare. I met with a personal trainer every day, and we focused on weight training, especially for leg strengthening exercises. I did countless squats and kettlebell movements, all the while knowing I had to be careful because I didn't want to push myself to the point of getting hurt right before the trip.

I also hired a climbing coach to help me gain as much mountaineering experience as I could in the little time I had. He taught me the "rest step," a way of walking to help preserve the most energy while going up the mountain. This involves pausing and locking out your back knee so that your leg is fully vertical. Then, you relax your bent front leg, relieving your leg muscles. I also learned how to save myself with an ice axe, a technique called self-arrest in which you slide down a snow bank, flip onto your stomach, and jab your ice axe into the snow to catch yourself if you're falling. Before I met my climbing coach in person, I told him I wanted mountaineer training for the Seven Summits. I didn't want to tell him I was going to Everest because I feared he would judge my experience level and tell me I wasn't ready. When I walked in the office, though, he surprised me with that very question.

"So, you're going to climb Everest?" he asked. I was caught completely off guard and wondered how could he possibly know.

"Huh?" I uttered shyly, with a confused look on my face.

"Well, you said you want to climb the Seven Summits, and Everest is one of them," he replied.

"Oh my gosh," I said. "I thought you actually knew I was going to climb Everest in a couple weeks!"

He was definitely surprised, but it was great because I had learned he had climbed Everest several years prior. His advice and coaching were well-targeted. I asked him if he thought I was completely crazy for saying yes and going. He told me that I wasn't crazy, but that I also needed to be mentally prepared in case I was simply too scared. He added that it was okay to just leave if it came down to that, reminding me Everest would always be there.

During those short weeks of preparation, I also worked with a sports psychologist. He discussed the mental part of the climb and asked if I was scared of any particular aspect. The only fear I could think of was dying in an avalanche, so we did several visualization activities to try to remove that fear. The psychologist instructed me to picture myself in an avalanche and visualize myself surviving it, playing the images back in my mind over and over from beginning to end. My fears weren't unjustified; of all the mountains of the Seven Summits, Everest was one of the most dangerous. The weather is such a variable that during climbing season the optimal window for summiting are the middle two weeks of May. After that time, monsoon season hits. Mother Nature doesn't play when it comes to Everest: the 2014 climbing season came to a halt due to an avalanche allowing very few summits that year. And in 2015, the devastating earthquake resulted in zero summits from either side of the mountain. The year I went, 2016, would be the first time in three years that normal climbing activity resumed on Everest.

For this climb, I definitely required more gear. Everest is a different breed, so I needed to special order a series of items online: a giant down snowsuit, immense down mitts, and triple layer boots you wear only if you're climbing Everest or another of the world's highest peaks. Everest boots are different in that they're both warm and lightweight. To break in my boots, I wore them everywhere—including near the seawall by my house. I can picture it now: a beautiful sunny day in Vancouver, and I'm walking around the seawall, at sea level, wearing knee-high, bright yellow Everest mountaineering boots— major style points, eh?

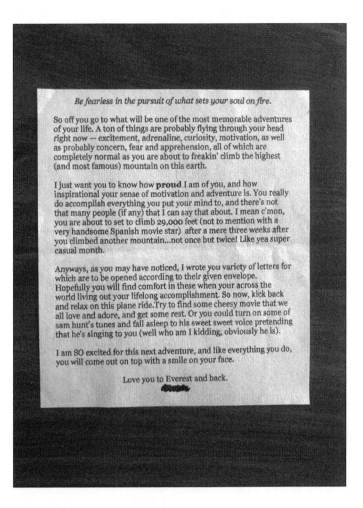

Be fearless in the pursuit of what sets your soul on fire.

So off you go to what will be one of the most memorable adventures of your life. A ton of things are probably flying through your head right now — excitement, adrenaline, curiosity, motivation, as well as probably concern, fear and apprehension, all of which are completely normal as you are about to freakin' climb the highest (and most famous) mountain on this earth.

I just want you to know how **proud** I am of you, and how inspirational your sense of motivation and adventure is. You really do accomplish everything you put your mind to, and there's not that many people (if any) that I can say that about. I mean c'mon, you are about to set to climb 29,000 feet (not to mention with a very handsome Spanish movie star) after a mere three weeks after you climbed another mountain...not once but twice! Like yea super casual month.

Anyways, as you may have noticed, I wrote you variety of letters for which are to be opened according to their given envelope. Hopefully you will find comfort in these when your across the world living out your lifelong accomplishment. So now, kick back and relax on this plane ride.Try to find some cheesy movie that we all love and adore, and get some rest. Or you could turn on some of sam hunt's tunes and fall asleep to his sweet sweet voice pretending that he's singing to you (well who am I kidding, obviously he is).

I am SO excited for this next adventure, and like everything you do, you will come out on top with a smile on your face.

Love you to Everest and back.

THE MOUNTAIN AND THE GROUP

The majority of people climbing Everest approach it from the south side in Nepal, an area I'd visited before when my mom and I hiked to Everest Base Camp. My group took a different route, approaching the mountain from Tibet, known as the north side. The appealing aspect to many people about climbing from Tibet is that there is no "ice fall" like there is on the Nepal side. The ice fall—one of the most dangerous parts of the mountain—is a vast area of constantly shifting glacier chunks and endless crevasses with metal ladders strewn across for climbers to use as they very carefully cross over.

We were one of the first teams allowed into Tibet to start our journey to Base Camp. Several other teams had to start acclimatizing in Nepal because they weren't allowed in the country yet. In fact, more people would climb from Tibet if it weren't for the strict regulations. The Chinese government makes it complicated and difficult to get team permits to climb from Tibet, but our lead Sherpa was lucky and had gotten all our paperwork approved. I've heard sometimes it simply comes down to luck; the government can say no for absolutely no reason.

That said, there are downsides of approaching from Tibet, too. For example, there are no helicopters for rescue on the Tibet side like there are on the Nepal side. I tried not to think about the fact that it was a six-hour drive to the nearest hospital and instead focused on the big picture. There were pros and cons to each side, and I didn't have any say in what side my group chose because I had joined at the last minute.

I flew into Kathmandu and met up with the group: Star;

a woman in her forties who didn't speak any English; her personal guide; a man in his early forties; and a man from Mexico who had climbed from the Nepal side but was trying to summit from the Tibet side without oxygen. Everyone spoke Spanish...except for me.

We stayed in Kathmandu for a few days before flying to Lhasa, Tibet. From there, we drove ten days to get to Base Camp, but we didn't drive straight through. In fact, it was quite the opposite. Because we were driving instead of hiking to almost 17,000 feet, we had to travel extra slowly to help our bodies acclimatize. We stopped in little towns, did short day hikes, and stayed overnight in certain places along the way. The drive was long; we spent about eight hours a day in the car on those ride days, and I listened to music most of the time because I didn't understand the Spanish being spoken around me.

THE ASCENT

The acclimatization process is extremely important when it comes to Everest. For most people climbing Everest, the round-trip time for the adventure is about two months, no matter your experience level. A body coming from sea level needs plenty of time to acclimatize.

Climbing Everest happens in three rotations: first, climbers reach a designated point and then come back down to Base Camp and rest. The second rotation is the same, except that climbers reach a higher point before coming down again to rest. The third rotation is the summit push. Even though the climb from Base Camp to the summit takes just five days, it's imperative to go slowly to enable your body to adapt to the altitude. How imperative? If a helicopter took an unacclimatized climber from sea level to the top of Everest and just dropped them off, that climber would get a spectacular view, but they'd live for only about seven minutes.

From the north side (Tibet) our climb was broken down as follows:

- Base Camp: 16,900 ft. (5151 m)
- Intermediate Camp: 20,300 ft. (6187 m)
- ABC: Advanced Base Camp: 21,300 ft. (6492 m)
- Camp One: The North Col: 23,000 ft. (7000 m)
- Camp Two: 24,750 ft. (7500 m)
- Camp Three: 27,390 ft. (8300 m) (In the death zone)

Before you start climbing Everest, a Puja ceremony is held to bless the climbers and all the climbing gear for a safe passage on the mountain. Three lamas, spiritual leaders in Buddhism, perform the ceremony, singing, dancing, praying, and chanting. The leaders of the ceremony toss Tibetan cooking flour into the air and rub it on the faces of the climbers and Sherpas for good luck.

The ceremony is a way to show respect to the mountain, which is a pivotal part of the culture and experience of climbing Mount Everest.

FIRST ROTATION

Our team's objective for the first rotation was to touch the bottom of the North Col (the area on the mountain where the fixed ropes start). After acclimatizing at Base Camp for a few days, it was time to start. On day one, we intended to hike from Base Camp to Intermediate Camp and spend the night back at Base Camp—but there was one problem. That morning, I woke up with an altitude-induced headache. Our doctor advised I just stay at Base Camp. Because we'd taken so long to get to the start of our first rotation, I was reluctant and heartbroken to be left behind. My team assured me it was only one day and we had nearly two months of climbing to follow. The next day, I was feeling a bit better but still not fully myself. The plan was to hike to Intermediate Camp and sleep there. I started out following the long, rocky path with the rest of my team, which also involved constantly getting out of the way of yaks carrying the gear of all the climbers on the mountain. About an hour in, I was turned back by the doctor. Feeling nauseated, I could not move quickly enough. I wiped my tears and headed back to Base Camp. It was an awful start to the trip, and I was feeling mentally defeated. All this time, all this way, and I couldn't be starting off on a worse foot. I also felt pressure to show everyone, including myself, that despite lacking extensive experience, I could succeed. Besides the chef and a couple Sherpas, I was the only one left in Base Camp. I had a gourmet meal consisting of ramen noodles, Coca-Cola, and Pringles that night for dinner and headed straight to bed. Finally, the third day, a Sherpa was able to take me to rejoin my team at Intermediate Camp. We spent the night there and continued the long, rocky journey to Advanced Base Camp.

Advanced Base Camp, commonly referred to as ABC, sits at 21,300 feet—higher than the top of Mount Kilimanjaro—and is a tent city similar to Base Camp; however, it sprawls over uneven, rocky terrain and doesn't have all the luxuries of Base Camp. That said, it still has a toilet, dining tent, and Wi-Fi—all luxuries in my book. My first night sleeping at ABC, I was the sickest I've ever been in my entire life. I woke up in the middle of the night with a horrible headache and couldn't stop vomiting. It was freezing—so cold, in fact, that when I woke up again to be sick, I was vomiting onto my now-frozen previous vomit in a container I kept for emergencies in my tent. The next night, I asked our team doctor to sleep in my tent because I was scared I was going to be severely ill again; thankfully, I ended up feeling better that night. ABC was the highest altitude I had ever camped at, and I learned the hard way how difficult it is to sleep at this altitude.

From ABC, we continued up and finally reached the glacier. Until this point, we had worn hiking boots, but now we were at "crampon point"—where everyone puts their crampons on their mountaineering boots and gets into their harnesses. In other words, it's where the actual climbing begins. My Sherpa roped me to him to protect me from hidden crevasses—deep cracks in the glacier covered by snow—and we crossed the glacier to where the fixed ropes started, leading from that point all the way to the summit of Everest. After a couple more nights sleeping at ABC, our first rotation was complete. We made our way back down to Base Camp to rest and recover for our second rotation.

BASE CAMP LIFE

For me, a typical day at Base Camp consisted of waking up super early. When the sun hit the tent, it became a sauna, and I was forced to get out because I felt desperate for fresh air—that was, on sunny days. Then, we would meet as a team in the dining area, which had a large rectangular table seating about twelve people comfortably. Base Camp breakfasts ranged from pancakes to eggs and oatmeal, and cereal was always available. After that, the days were mine. I could walk around Base Camp for exercise or to socialize with the other teams—and the socialization, by the way, was sometimes like a big party scene. On a good day, I could wait my turn for a shower—a mix of hot and cold water, but what an indescribable feeling to get to be clean! I wrote in my journal as much as I could. I kept detailed journals on all of my climbs. I knew one day I would love looking back and reliving my adventures. I also found myself listening to a lot of music to fill my time, mostly my Spotify country playlists, as they were the only few that were pre-downloaded. By the end of the trip, let's just say Sam Hunt was rather overplayed. People were frustrated by the incredibly slow Wi-Fi. When I got the chance, I loved touching base with my family and friends back home, and when I didn't have the opportunity to talk to anyone, I opened letters that people had written before my trip. They were all labeled differently with qualifiers like "open at Camp One," "open when you need a hug," or "open before you leave for the summit." My mom wrote one that brought me to tears:

A note to my Beautiful baby girl...

Liz—

I do not know if I can get through writing this note without huge crocodile tears coming down my face. I want you to know that there will not be a day or a minute when I do not think about you. I miss you so much already!!

As I write this note you are out buying your last minute little bits of gear with Daddy, this past week you have seemed so happy and so excited. I am happy too that you are following your dream to conquer Everest.

Dad and I are so incredibly proud of you! You have lived your 25 years of life grabbing every opportunity that presents itself to you. You have seen the world by means of so many different journeys. Gumption should have been one of your middle names.

I do have to say that this journey that you are on right now terrifies me and I will not stop worrying about you until you are home in my arms. Please be careful my precious baby girl. Listen to your body and to your heart.

Remember...the story is not about the summit.

Enjoy the spectacular beauty of mother nature that surrounds you, have fun meeting all of those new people at Base Camp. Enjoy learning that beautiful Spanish language and remember that the people around you are so lucky to have You with them!

I will miss you my sweet girl. In the next cards that I write I will list everything that I will miss about not having my Liz home with me.

I love you to the moon and back a trillion times!

Be safe, Beautiful girl.

Love you forever,

Mom

"If you want your life to be a magnificent story, then begin by realizing that you are the author and every day you have the opportunity to write a new page." Liz...you are the best author of new pages!

SECOND ROTATION

The goal of the second rotation was to sleep at Camp One for two nights. We started from Base Camp, made our way to Intermediate Camp, and then to ABC. From there, we packed up our sleeping bags and put on our climbing gear. I was ecstatic to actually be headed up the mountain. The climb to Camp One was steep and quite crowded with other groups. I followed the ropes up and took it one step at a time. There was a lot of stopping and going because people were constantly unclipping and clipping into different sections of the rope—a technique that can cause delays in a steady pace. By the time I got to the top, I was thrilled to crawl into a pre-set-up tent and focus on getting warm.

After the first night at Camp One, we climbed toward Camp Two—an extremely difficult feat given the lack of oxygen. Every five steps, I wanted to take a break and sit in the snow. The guides assured us we would have oxygen at this stage on our final rotation, but not that day. The higher we went up without oxygen on this rotation, the better our bodies would acclimatize, they explained. The climb was incredibly difficult; often, I'd look down the ridgeline and see fellow climbers sitting in the snow, just as I wanted to do so badly.

On the second night at Camp One, I was ill again and ended up vomiting *on* Star, who was trying to get me a bag (thank goodness we were already friends). We both suffered the next morning from lack of sleep and oxygen. While climbing back down to ABC, I still felt awful but I knew that because we had successfully slept at Camp One for two nights, we had our green light for the summit push (as it relates to acclimatization) and that rotation two was officially over.

The third rotation was the summit push, and the group and I wanted to stay at ABC until then rather than hike all the way back down to Base Camp. We hoped the ropes would be set in time for us to start our summit rotation but found out on the radio and through people from different teams that the Chinese government had no idea when they were going to set the ropes to the top. We heard it could be ten days, but it was anyone's guess, really. As a result, our hands were tied and we had to return to Base Camp. This was an awful trek to keep repeating and one we'd repeat six times over the course of the climb. Still, we knew we had to return to Base Camp instead of waiting out the time for the ropes to be set because the body simply can't recover well enough in ten days at such a high altitude.

After hiking down to Base Camp, I knew I needed to continue descending due to all the illness I'd suffered. With altitude sickness, the best thing to do is to go as low as possible; the body needs high levels of oxygen to recover.

Sea level would have been ideal, but on Everest, that's obviously not possible. When I found out we would be waiting days for the ropes to be set, I opted to travel to a 14,000-foot (4,330-meter) town called Shegar, where I got a hotel for three nights and a real bed. Comparatively speaking, it was an oxygen-rich environment.

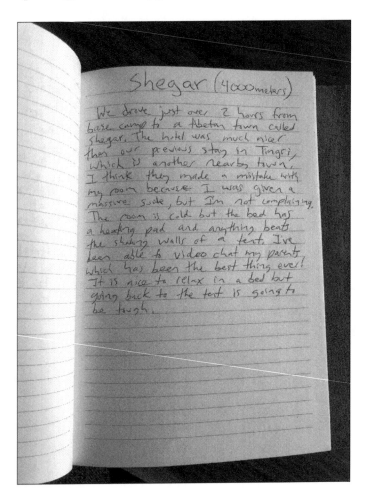

THIRD ROTATION

After recovering and reconvening at Base Camp, it was time to start the third rotation. We left and hiked to Intermediate Camp, spending one night there before climbing to ABC for another night. This was the last time we would have Wi-Fi until we were back here again. I connected with my dad late at night to say goodbye for now. It was incredibly early in the morning for him back in Vancouver. This was a routine we had established early on the trip because the Wi-Fi was better for me late at night when most people in my group had gone to bed.

To get my mind off worrying about not being able to connect with them for several days, I asked about what was going on back home and, as a welcomed distraction, he told me about his upcoming day. He had a meeting with the president of my favorite hockey team, the Vancouver Canucks, about a local charity that they were both involved with. I said, "Well, you tell 'him' (I used a nickname as if we were great buddies, when really, he had no clue who I was) that I'm taking the Canucks flag to the top of world!" My dad had no clue I had brought the flag with me but was thrilled to be able to pass on the message—and did so, using my nickname and all.

The next morning, we climbed to Camp One without oxygen and slept there for one night. On the following day we started using oxygen—a change that made the climb to Camp Two *so* much easier than it had been the first time. For the first time we slept with oxygen. I was initially nervous about falling asleep with a mask over my face, but it turned out to be no problem. I had the best night of sleep I'd had in days, and I sorely needed it.

The next day, we climbed up to Camp Three, arriving at about 5:00 p.m., but we didn't sleep. Instead, we rested, drank tea, and tried to relax before starting our summit push just five hours later.

Before the Everest trip, I had worried about using oxygen because it was new to me. During the first two rotations, we had practiced changing oxygen bottles and reading the regulators. We wore them for short periods to see what it felt like to walk with the masks over our mouths. After all that practice, I felt fine. My oxygen mask became my best friend and ultimately helped me reach my next destination: the summit.

THE SUMMIT

We left Camp Three at 10:00 p.m., about to attempt to summit the tallest mountain in the world. It was pitch dark and unbearably cold, and I was ready to move. In the freezing cold, knowing I was in the Death Zone, I couldn't help but feel impatient as my personal Sherpa helped get everyone else ready before he and I could go. As we began to move forward, I got nervous about my mitts. I didn't feel as though I had enough dexterity with the massive down mitts. I followed my intuition, and at the last minute, I switched to small Mountain Equipment Co-op ski gloves, packing my thicker mitts in the case of an emergency.

Minutes after we left the campsite, we came to a complete standstill, reaching a line of two hundred people, in the dark, wearing headlamps and all trying to move along the same rope. Wherever the rope was anchored into the snow, people got held up because they'd have to unclip their carabiner and their ascender to move on to the next rope. Everywhere I looked, I saw people waiting.

At one point, I recall moving along the rope, thinking about nothing aside from how dry my mouth was and how badly I wanted a candy to suck on. A drink. *Anything*. My mind wandered as we moved painstakingly slowly. All of a sudden, the climber in front of me slipped and fell, and his Sherpa went down with him. Neither of the men was hurt, but their fall was a powerful wake-up call. *Stop daydreaming about candy and focus, Liz.* After that, I was much more awake and concentrated on every single step.

At one point while it was still dark out, my oxygen mask started to freeze. I didn't know what was happening at the time; I just knew it had become really hard to breathe. I asked my Sherpa to check my oxygen, and he assured me everything was fine. But everything wasn't fine.

After a few moments, I couldn't breathe at all, so I took off my mask.

"What are you doing!?" my Sherpa asked, upset. "You have to put that back on!"

"There's no airflow," I said again. "I can't breathe at all."

Pushing to summit the highest peak in the world and not being able to breathe through your oxygen mask is a rather terrifying feeling. My Sherpa examined the mask closely and found it to be completely iced over. Thank goodness he was prepared; he had some hot water in his pack and poured it over the mask to unfreeze it. I kept reassuring myself that everything was going to be okay either way, as other climbers in our group had extra regulators in case one broke. Nonetheless, it was still a scary moment.

After continuing for hours in the dark, the sunrise was not only gorgeous, it was welcome. The surrounding mountain peaks were lit with an array of golden colors across the sky. Before the sun came up, I looked and felt as though I had stepped out of a deep freezer; when the sun came up, it was instantly warmer, melting my iced-over wisps of hair.

We continued climbing in daylight for a while and finally summited at 10:47 that morning, more than twelve hours after we'd left Camp Three. To reach the summit, I had to unclip from the ropes that had taken me from the bottom of the mountain to the top. Standing at the top of the world's tallest mountain, I wasn't attached to anything besides my Sherpa, who was holding onto the clip now.

The summit area was small and sketchy, no bigger than the average dining room table. I was told by my Sherpa that some surrounding ice ledges were about to break off—not all that comforting. But still, nothing could take away from the beautiful sight draped in flags—prayer flags, flags of various nations, and personal flags of all kinds. I wanted to take more photographs, but my poor Sherpa was getting frostbite from trying to take all of the pictures I wanted. I posed with a Canadian flag and my Canucks flag proudly on top of the world. We stayed at the summit for about forty-five minutes (although most climbers don't stay that long). I wanted to wait for Star, but my Sherpa said he could see the weather turning, and we needed to leave. You go down the same way you go up, so I was able to high-five the rest of my group as I descended.

THE DESCENT

Summiting Mount Everest was a feat, but I didn't want to get ahead of myself; I knew I had another feat in front of me: getting down. There was only one rope going up and down the mountain, so my Sherpa and I had to unclip and maneuver around other climbers in order to pass by them. This process required me to put my trust in complete strangers who were as oxygen-deprived as I was. Passing by climbers who were on their ascent, I needed to unclip from the rope and hand them my leash so that they could move around it. That arrangement meant they were often the ones who re-clipped me back onto the rope—in other words, my lifeline.

The first and second steps were giant rock cliffs I had to rappel down, using a belay device and my hand as a brake. Other sections were so narrow I could barely fit one foot on the mountain when I moved around rock corners. In those places, I found myself hanging from the rope and stepped as carefully as I could. Here, I learned quickly that my crampons would do me no good on the rocky terrain; they're truly only meant for snow and ice. Rocks are tricky and crampons slip—and slip I did, slicing my Sherpa's snowsuit in the process. Overall, the climb down was a completely different scenario from the climb up. Before the climb, I had been warned that most of the accidents happen on the way down, so mentally, I was nervous. For me, descending Everest was scarier than ascending.

After I passed the first few unnerving spots, my energy switched to excitement. I was anxious to get down to Camp Three as fast as I could and finally get some rest. Plus, it had occurred to me that I had not gone to the bathroom for over twenty-four hours!

As we made our way down, the lead Sherpa asked my Sherpa to stay and wait for the other group members and help make sure they got down safely. Then the lead Sherpa took Star and me back to camp.

As we were climbing down, Star started out super strong near the top and he helped calm my nerves about descending. And then he hit a wall. He began to show major signs of fatigue. He'd take five steps and sit in the snow, absolutely exhausted and unable to function. Because of the altitude, he wasn't thinking clearly; his decision-making abilities were totally off. Eventually, he could only take two steps before his body needed to stop. The Sherpa and I tried to remain kind and encouraging, reminding him to think of his gorgeous wife and his three beautiful children and to keep moving for them.

"Honestly, I just need to sleep," he said. "I know where the campsite is. I'm going to sleep for forty-five minutes and then I'm going to meet you there."

"No, you can't sleep," I told him. "You're coming with us, and then you can sleep in the tent."

"No! I need sleep!" he said, beginning to show signs of anger and frustration.

At that point, I was done being nice because I knew he was in danger. "You know what?" I screamed. "Have you seen the *Everest* movie? Everyone dies. I'm twenty-five and I'm too young to die! Now get up! Let's go. Do it for your wife and kids!"

The Sherpa attached him to a rope and practically pulled him down the mountain because he was walking so slowly. We finally got him to Camp Three. I knew he was mad at me, but I didn't care.

First thing the next morning, Star found me. "Liz, you never left me," he said.

"No kidding!" I said, smiling. "I wasn't about to leave you on Everest!"

After spending the night at Camp Three, we climbed all the way down to ABC fighting against the most powerful windstorm I'd ever seen or felt. If we hadn't been attached to the rope, we might very well have flown off of the mountain. At one point, we took cover in our broken tent at Camp Two; everything had been destroyed. Two out of four of our tents were still standing—but barely.

Eventually, we made it down to Camp One. At that point, I simply *had* to reach ABC. I *needed* to get off the mountain, talk to my parents, and have a good night's sleep. I learned later that five people had died while I was up there. My family and friends back home were frantic watching the news on TV, waiting to hear from me. The deaths took place on the other side of the mountain, however, this was not clear on the news.

It's hard to articulate my emotions coming off of Everest, even in retrospect. I learned some of the most valuable and challenging lessons life could have presented me with. I pushed myself farther than I had expected to go, and I proved to myself that I am stronger than I ever believed. But when it was all said and done, it was an experience I wouldn't wish upon my future children or any of my loved ones.

BELIEVE IN YOURSELF

Was climbing Everest easy mentally? Absolutely not—but I had to have faith in my ability to persevere. Whether you're climbing a mountain or pursuing your own passion, self-doubt will only betray you. If Everest were easy, it wouldn't be such an amazing feat. The toughest situations are often the most rewarding, and it's important to keep your mental game strong when powering through things that are hard physically, emotionally, or otherwise.

KEEP THE BIGGER GOAL IN MIND

During the setbacks like getting sick and climbing the sketchy parts of the mountain, I was able to power through and remain positive by keeping the bigger goal in mind. Not many people can say they've summitted Everest, and in the back of my mind, I knew I was going to be one of them. The same goes for you; take incremental steps to reach your goals, but never lose sight of the big win at the end. It will help you persevere through the tough days.

USE—AND ACTIVELY SEEK OUT— POSITIVITY AND MOTIVATION

On Everest, I talked to myself to keep going, but I also relied on the encouragement of others. I celebrated my birthday right before I left for Everest, and I asked everyone for letters to open throughout various points on my two-month journey. I received over forty letters with instructions about when to open them, and the inspirational messages kept me going as much as my own positive self-talk.

Chapter 6

16,050 ft. (4,892 m) above Sea Level

We don't meet people by accident. They are meant to cross our path for a reason.

—UNKNOWN

For the first few weeks after I'd climbed Mount Everest, I was on top of the world. I felt lucky Everest was only my third of the Seven Summits because if I had ended with Everest, I can't help but think I would have struggled with a "now what?" feeling. Instead, I was happy to have a bigger goal in mind. After taking the summer to be with friends and family, I got a job with a local Vancouver company specializing in climbing apparel called Arc'teryx. I set my sights on the next step in reaching my Seven Summit goal: Mount Vinson in Antarctica.

PREPARATION

Mount Vinson is the second lowest of the Seven Summits, but it feels higher because of how cold and remote it is. Although I'd just come from Everest, I didn't approach Vinson thinking it would be overly easy. There were unique factors for which I had to prepare. For example, Vinson can be colder than Everest, and the environment is harsh. In addition, there are no porters or Sherpas to carry the gear; Mount Vinson would be my first experience carrying all of my gear, so I had to train a bit differently. I did exercises with heavy weights to make sure I could carry the necessary weight in my backpack.

There was another factor to consider, too: on Vinson, you can't fit everything in your backpack for the lower portion of the mountain, so you fill a classic children's tobogganing sled with all your gear, roping it in so nothing falls out and rigging it to your backpack. To prepare for this challenge, my trainer had me pull heavy objects from one end of the gym to the other, representing what it would be like hauling the sled up and down the mountain.

THE MOUNTAIN AND THE GROUP

I was excited as I flew from Vancouver to Punta Arenas, Chile, where I met my group and had an orientation and gear check. Landing on a glacier in Antarctica is tricky, so we waited for perfect weather to fly the rest of the way. There can be no fog at all. Once the weather cleared, we flew on a large Russian jet that felt more like a cargo plane. Everything was exposed, with wires dangling from the ceiling of the plane. We carried on our own luggage and piled it in the back of the plane. There were no windows, but there was a television screen inside on which we could watch the landing on the icy runway, which happens to be positioned on one of the windiest parts of the continent (Interestingly enough, this is intentional: the powerful wind acts as a natural snow removal system to keep the runway clear).

To keep our bodies from going into shock once we deplaned, the plane itself was kept at a very low temperature, so we were advised to wear our heavy mountaineering gear while aboard. Upon landing, we were welcomed with bitter wind and indescribable cold. I tried to take off my glove to snap a few photos of the plane, but it took about ten seconds until I couldn't feel my fingers anymore. Welcome to Antarctica!

Our group for this ten-day adventure consisted of five people: two men in their forties who were best friends; my tent-mate, who was in her late fifties; and a younger man around my age. The best friends were ultra-marathon runners (let's call them the Ultra Bros) who were ridiculously cocky yet fun guys to be around. They had climbed a few of the Seven Summits, but not Everest or Denali, which are the more serious climbs. My tent-mate was from Connecticut and didn't have much climbing experience, but she was kind and thrilled to be in Antarctica. Like me, the fellow my age was also trying to climb the Seven Summits, and this was his fourth climb. Our American guide was very well-known in the mountaineering world. Though I hadn't heard of him before the trip, I soon learned he had climbed the Seven Summits ten times, often referring to his accomplishment as the "seventy summits."

I quickly bonded with him and everyone in my group. In such an intense situation, it's common to go from "Hi, my name is Liz" to "Were you able to poop today?" within twenty-four hours. That's one of the special things about these expeditions: you become close with your group *very* quickly, whether you like it or not.

On all my other climbs, I had worried I would be the least experienced. This time, however, because I had just come from Everest, I was highly confident. I knew Vinson would be a challenge but one I could handle. I was the youngest member of our group, but I felt like I was the most qualified for the climb.

THE ASCENT

Our plane landed on Union Glacier, and from there we took a Twin Otter ski plane to Base Camp. From there, we piled up our sleds and climbed to Camp One. We were all roped together on a rope team—a first for me. On Everest, I had been roped to the mountain, but I had never been attached to other people. We climbed in a rope team because we crossed glaciers and being connected to one another meant we could stop someone from falling if they slipped as we crossed.

Antarctica has twenty-four hours of daylight in January, meaning sleeping was tricky. I ended up putting a neck warmer over my eyes, but it was still a foreign concept for me.

Another challenge was the bathroom situation. We could dump pee bottles only at the yellow flags planted in the snow, so the men just peed at the flags. We had plastic bags for poop. At Base Camp and Camp One, we had a communal bucket with a plastic bag in it, and a toilet seat that sat on top. For the rest of the mountain, we each carried and used our own plastic poop bags, carrying these from camp to camp. Base Camp had three makeshift bathrooms made out of low ice-brick walls (three stalls, to be exact). One was for pooping, and the other two were for the girls to have some privacy while they used their pee bottles.

I was grateful for this privacy. Using a pee bottle was still new for me, though I'd practiced before the trip. On the first day, I used one of the shelters to pee into my bottle. When I looked down, I realized I had completely missed. One of the Ultra Bros was in the stall next to me, sitting on the toilet. We had known each other for twenty-four hours.

I called his name shyly. "I missed," I said over the ice wall. "My bottle is empty."

"It's okay, don't worry," he said.

"What do I do?" I asked.

"I don't know," he said. "Just bury it with snow."

"Are you sure?" I said.

"Yeah," he replied. "Do you want me to help you?"

"No!" I said. "I've got it. Thanks, though."

Later, I watched men from other groups walk right to up the pee flag and go to the bathroom. I turned to my guide.

"Is there any way I can just squat next to the flag like the guys, instead of using the bottle?" I asked.

"Yeah," he replied. "If you're comfortable with that, go for it."

And so I did, for the rest of the trip.

We pulled our sleds from Base Camp to Low Camp. From here, a section of fixed ropes would take us to High Camp. No one else in the Vinson group had used fixed lines before, but I had just spent all Everest season getting acquainted with the process.

Because Vinson is at a much lower altitude, this part of the climb felt like a walk in the park. I attached my ascender and wanted to run up the whole thing because I was used to using the ropes at 28,000 feet and going so slowly. I was confident about moving up quickly, but everyone else in my group found it really challenging. We carried half of our gear to the top of the fixed ropes and stored it in the snow, climbing back down to sleep at Camp One. The next day, we packed up our tents and the rest of our gear and moved everything up to High Camp. So far, so smooth.

THE SUMMIT

On summit day, we woke early to a perfectly sunny day. There was not a single cloud in the sky. We followed the trail and summited in two rope teams. Because there wasn't a steep incline at this point and we didn't need our ice axes yet, I used ski poles to help with stability while walking at the very end of the second rope team. To entertain myself, I took one of my poles and started writing my name and drawing hearts in the snow.

On a rope team, you have to keep the rope at a consistent level of tension; it can't be too tight or too loose. I started playing a game with myself to see what I could draw in the snow while keeping the perfect rope tension. Then, I realized one more team would be climbing Vinson that season, too, so I started writing them inspirational messages in the snow. I wrote messages like, "You can do it" and "Drink lots of water" and "Way to go!" I also wrote "O Canada!" more times than I can count.

At one point, we stopped to gear up for the summit ridge—a sketchier part of the climb that required walking along a thin ridgeline with drops on either side. One of the climbers on our team had a panic attack right before the ridgeline and began to hyperventilate and cry. After the situation calmed down, I led one rope team along the summit ridgeline, as our guide led the other.

Earlier that day, this particular climber had wanted to quit. Instead of letting it happen, the guide took the climber's backpack and pushed them to keep going, something I know they didn't regret, especially after experiencing the view from the top. Summit day was an inexplicably perfect day; everywhere I looked, I saw beautiful white mountaintops. We took photos at the summit before climbing back down to High Camp to sleep. The next day, we climbed down to Base Camp and at that point, we were ready to leave. However, to get back to Union Glacier, the plane needed perfect weather, a rarity in Antarctica. That day, the weather wasn't perfect, so the plane wasn't waiting for us at Base Camp as we had hoped. We spent the night at camp and waited for the plane to pick us up the next day.

When we returned to Union Glacier, we sat in the communal tent drinking hot chocolate. Soon, the team that had been climbing behind us arrived. I didn't know anyone on the team, but I leaned over to their table and asked, "Hey guys. Did you get my messages in the snow?"

"Oh, that was you?" a climber asked.

"Yeah!" I said.

"I liked the 'O Canada' ones," he said.

"Oh, yeah?" I said. "Are you from Canada?"

"Yeah, I'm from Calgary," he said. "I'm Hockey (a nickname for the purposes of this book). Nice to meet you."

After that, Hockey and I became buddies. At that point, I didn't have a flight home because I wasn't sure when the climb was going to end. Hockey told me when his flight was and suggested I try to get on it, which I did. I learned he owned a heli-skiing company, and I told him I worked for Arc'teryx, a climbing company, and then I suggested he and I trade gear for heli-skiing. He loved the idea.

As I stood in a coffee line later at the airport, Hockey came up behind me, and I bought his drink. He asked for my number so we could stay in touch.

"Do you have Instagram or Facebook or anything fun?" I asked.

"Actually, I own a hockey team," Hockey replied, "so the league does that for me."

Only then did I learn he is the owner of an NHL team and a major player in the business world. We ended up having many mutual friends; what a small world! In March of that year, Hockey set me up to go heli-skiing for my birthday and we also planned to share future climbs together.

I met someone besides Hockey while at Union Glacier waiting for the plane. By "met," I mean I saw a man who would capture my attention beyond anything I would ever expect. I had no idea who he was; I didn't know if he was a random climber, a guide, or an employee. I overheard him introduced as a guide. Being shy, I didn't introduce myself, but at dinner, I turned to my tentmate and whispered, "The other group's guide is so cute!" He was six feet tall with brown hair, an athletic build, faint freckles, and nice eyes.

"Do you know who that is?" she asked.

"A guide?" I said, oblivious.

"No! He owns the mountaineering company and is a

famous guide!" she said, as if I should have known who he was. I didn't have a clue.

"Oh, perfect," I said. "He can take me on another climb!"

I never did introduce myself at Union Glacier, but when I got home, I added him on social media and asked if he would guide me on Mount Elbrus, sixth on my list of the Seven Summits. He agreed; from there, we began to plan our trip.

FOCUS ON CONNECTING

You never know where your connections might lead, so don't be afraid to reach out to new people. In life, the more people you know, the higher the likelihood that opportunities will open for you. No matter what your passion is, remember that it's a small world. Get to know as many people as you can.

RECOGNIZE THE BEAUTY AROUND YOU

Mount Vinson was one of my favorites of the Seven Summits because it was clean and pristine. The relatively untouched beauty of Antarctica in general took my breath away. I could have focused on the challenge or the cold, but instead I kept my eyes open and focused on the beautiful view—something you can do in your own life. You don't have to be in Antarctica to seek out and celebrate the beauty around you.

Chapter 7

20,310 ft. (6,190 m) above Sea Level

Many of life's failures are people who didn't realize how close they were to success when they gave up.

—THOMAS EDISON

After climbing Mount Vinson, I had five months until Denali climbing season, which runs from May until the end of June. During that time, I worked for Arc'teryx and began training for my next climb: Denali, the hardest summit in terms of backpacking weight.

PREPARATION

Back when Star and I were on our way to Everest, we decided we would climb Denali together with his guide, whom I had met in Argentina. The guide had agreed to the Denali climb but, understandably, told us to focus on Everest first.

Researching Denali, I found there were only six approved companies legally able to guide on the mountain. It's a national park and the rules are strict. While anyone can get a permit and climb, it's illegal to pay someone outside of the six companies to guide you. Star, his guide, and I were going to say we were climbing as friends in order to get around the issue of legality, but something in my gut didn't feel comfortable climbing that way. At this point, I learned that Star was unable to make the trip. I felt a huge moral dilemma inside of me; I didn't want to let anyone down or ruin any relationships, but I knew it was ethically wrong. I needed to reach my Seven Summit goal the right way, so when I put my head on the pillow at night, I felt proud about it. On top of that, Denali is a massive climb with an abundance of issues of its own. The last thing I wanted to stress about was getting kicked off the mountain because I hadn't followed the rules. I hated bailing on Star's friend, but I explained the situation, and we parted on good terms. Shortly after, I chose a guide from one of the companies approved to lead climbers on Denali.

I trained hard for Denali, knowing well it was going to be a challenge for me to carry three weeks of gear and food up the mountain. I spent a lot of time in the gym focusing on heavy lifting and cardio-based workouts, and I went on as many local hikes as I could to practice carrying a heavy pack. As my training progressed, I kept adding more and more weight to my pack.

THE MOUNTAIN AND THE GROUP

I flew from Vancouver to Anchorage before taking a train to a small town called Talkeetna, the launch point for anyone climbing Denali. After I arrived, our group had to get our permits and meet with the park board services. The park board talked our group through mountain safety on Denali and all of the rules of the road: how to dispose of waste, national park etiquette, and what steps to take in case of an emergency. Once the talk was over, our guides had us do a thorough gear check and took us to the next location to pack our food for the next three weeks. Enter: The Snack Room. The Snack Room was one of the most glorious sights I've ever set my eyes on, a room filled to the brim with any snack you could possibly want: candy bars, goldfish, cookies, nuts, trail mix, beef jerky, you name it. I felt like a kid in a candy store. We had three bags to fill: first week, second week, third week. We quickly filled our food bags and made sure we had everything we needed for the next twenty-one days on the glacier.

This was the first time I would be the only female in my group, an intentional choice on my part. The four men in my group included two older men, a sixty-seven-year-old and another who claimed he had stopped counting his age at thirty-six. He was actually in his fifties, but we'll call him Thirty-Six. My tentmates were two younger guys, one guy from Minnesota and one from California; we'll call them Minnesota and Red (a nickname referring to his hair color). They said it was fine to bunk with them as long as I didn't mind them smoking weed. (I thought they were joking but soon learned they weren't.)

Thirty-Six had already tried to climb Denali twice. One time, he had gotten sick, and the other time, he simply wasn't fit enough. He was hoping to summit on his third try. Minnesota had taken a mountaineering course the previous summer from the same company we were using as our guides. He hadn't climbed any big peaks but thought he'd attempt Denali. Red had climbed several fourteeners—mountains above 14,000 feet—in

Colorado, but those were day trips. This was his first expedition-style mountaineering trip. From a climbing resume perspective, I was by far the most experienced group member.

I knew Denali would be an interesting journey. The tallest US mountains are in Alaska, and Denali is the highest at 20,310 feet. While Everest is the highest mountain in the world, Denali has the highest elevation gain from starting altitude to the summit. We allowed a twenty-one-day time frame to climb Denali. Technically, we could have done it in fewer days, but we gave ourselves extra time since the weather is unpredictable. Like Aconcagua, Denali has a reputation of having bad weather. I knew that of all the Seven Summits, Denali was the one I would most likely have to repeat due to bad weather; many teams end up not summiting because snowstorms prevent them from moving past a certain camp. Before I left, I tried to sign up for back-to-back trips to cover my bases. In the end, the company wouldn't let me sign up for both without paying for the full amount for both, so I decided it would be wiser to wait and see how it played out.

I wanted Mount Kosciuszko in Australia to be my last mountain of the Seven Summits because I was going to do it with family and friends, and it would be the easiest, as it is more of a walk than a climb. But if I was denied my first attempt to summit Denali, I knew I'd have to wait another year to try again. Not being able to plan Australia until I had completed Denali, I was anxious to do so on my first attempt if my hope was to achieve my goal in the timeline I envisioned.

THE ASCENT

Similar to Mount Vinson, we traveled to Base Camp in a Twin Otter ski plane—a small plane with oversized ski blades for landing on glaciers. The plane carried our group plus all of our gear, and trust me, there was *a lot* of gear. Just as on Mount Vinson, our Denali group carried both personal gear as well as group gear such as tents, cooking equipment, and food. Between my backpack and my sled, I carried about 120 pounds of gear my first day on Denali.

When we arrived in the afternoon, our guide told us we were leaving "at two." He didn't clarify as to whether he meant two in the morning or in the afternoon; he just said two. Naturally, I thought we were leaving at two in the afternoon. *Nope.* We left at two in the morning, when it was still dark and the glacier was still frozen. During the summer in Alaska, there are only three to four hours of such darkness and it is important to take advantage of them. As soon as the sun comes out, it gets unbearably hot and turns the glacier into a coat of thick slush, making it treacherous to cross and navigate. After I had experienced that, I definitely understood why we'd left so early.

Mount Vinson was the perfect mountain to climb before Denali because it gave me experience climbing in a rope team and pulling a sled. Crossing the glacier involved moving over seemingly endless crevasses—cracks in the ice that are so deep, you can't see the bottom. To navigate the crevasses, we would find the narrowest point and the whole rope team would stop at the edge. These are the moments you have to fully and undoubtedly trust your teammates, even when you're overwhelmed with fear. We'd count to three as one person at a time jumped across, the person in front of them pulling the rope to make sure the person behind didn't fall in. We were all attached to the rope, so every move impacted the whole team. There were moments when I truly felt raw with fear. Crossing the first crevasse, I tried to keep my eyes straight ahead and just take a big step, not focusing on what was below. What didn't help my fear was seeing people from other climbing groups struggling nearby, half of their bodies dangling over the crevasse, their arms gripping onto the snow, trying not to fall in.

The first day on Denali was brutal. When you drag a sled, you're supposed to drag it directly behind you. For some reason, my sled kept veering off to the side, and by the time we got to camp that night, my shoulder was overwhelmed with a dull pain that I couldn't shake. I immediately felt defeated; I had twenty more days left on this mountain, and I seemed to have hurt myself on the first day. How was I going to get through the next three weeks? Thankfully, my shoulder ended up feeling much better the next day. It was a good thing, too, because as the trip continued, the two older climbers—Sixty-Seven and Thirty-Six—couldn't carry any group gear; they could barely carry their own. That left me, Minnesota, and Red to pick up the slack and carry the gear for everyone.

STUCK AT 11,000 CAMP

On Denali, the camps are referred to by their elevation; Camp Two, for example, is called 11,000 Camp. We were stuck at 11,000 Camp for eleven days, and it snowed for eight of them. Lying in a small tent, crammed with gear for three grown adults, with two guys I barely knew, I went stir crazy. We had nothing to fill our days with as we waited out the weather, so we mostly just played music in our tent and snacked. Whisking together matcha tea (Thanks, Red!) and eating hummus and crackers will forever remind me of the inside of that orange and grey tent, coated with snow which we had to take turns brushing off. While the matcha and hummus probably paints a cozy picture of our time in the tent, don't be fooled. We were, after all, on a glacier, and it was *freezing*. Every day, we would wake up hopeful, only to be told by our guide that we wouldn't be going anywhere. During that period, we didn't even put on our mountaineering boots. We'd leave our tents for breakfast, eat, and then go back in. The only time we left the tent was to pee, and sometimes I really had to push myself to do that because it was just too cold to want to unzip the tent. Every night before bed, I wrote in my journal—mostly just about meals and the weather during the days we didn't move.

Minnesota and Red stayed true to their word and did smoke weed every day, and I hung out listening to music and chilling. One of the days, I woke up with a headache, so even though the guys were generally really good about opening the tent to blow out their smoke, I told them I had a headache and that I wouldn't be mad if they didn't blow the smoke out today. Red turned back to me and said, "Oh, you have a headache? We'll pull out the *good* stuff today." Alas, my headache dissipated, and I knew that experience would be one of the true bonding moments for me and the guys.

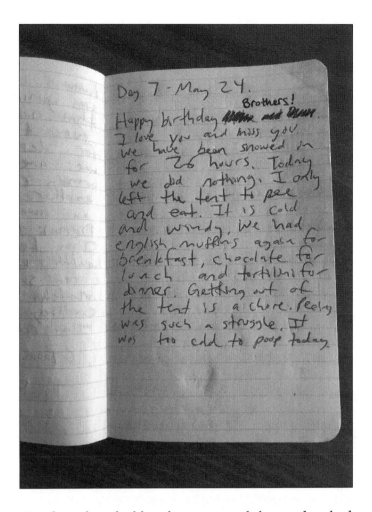

Day 7 - May 24.

Brothers!

Happy birthday ████ and ████. I love you and miss you. We have been snowed in for 26 hours. Today we did nothing. I only left the tent to pee and eat. It is cold and windy. We had english muffins again for breakfast, chocolate for lunch and tortillini for dinner. Getting out of the tent is a chore. Peeing was such a struggle. It was too cold to poop today.

One day, when the blue sky was crystal clear and we had no wind, we tried to move on. We spent hours packing up the entire campsite and got everything ready to move to the next campsite at 14,000 feet. After only a couple of short hours, we reached the top of Motorcycle Hill, which sits right above 11,000 Camp, but the mountain had other plans and the weather completely turned. A snowstorm was on the horizon, and we had no other choice but to turn around.

Once we got back to 11,000 Camp, we had to unpack and set up all of our tents and establish our camp. This sounds easy, but picture trying to peg down a tent while being whipped around in what felt like hurricane-force winds. Thirty-Six ended up getting frostbite, primarily because he couldn't pull up the zippers on his jacket without taking his gloves fully off repeatedly, exposing his flesh to the elements. The frostbite affected all ten of his fingers, but his thumbs were the worst; they were already beginning to turn black. Our guides carefully bandaged him up and told him he couldn't go any farther. On his third Denali attempt, he was forced to turn back, again. We had to wait a few days to find a group using the same company on their way down, who could take him with them.

After Thirty-Six left, Sixty-Seven moved into our tent. We sent the other tent down with Thirty-Six to reduce the weight for our uphill journey. That meant another full-sized air mattress, another three weeks of gear, all in our already crowded tent. A couple nights later, when I couldn't handle being squished in the tent with now three grown men, I went to the kitchen tent, a long red half dome under which we dug out the bottom, enabling us to stand upright. At the end of the day, it meant more space than the overcrowded tent, so I took my sleeping bag, unzipped the red tent door, and slept on the floor for a couple nights.

I knew we were quickly approaching our "up or down" day—that is, the day we had to either move up the mountain to have enough days to summit and make it all the way back down or move down the mountain because we wouldn't have enough days to ascend and descend. Essentially, every day we stayed at 11,000 Camp was another summit day lost. As we counted down the lost days during the snowstorm, we were also counting lost chances. I spent time in the tent with tears streaming down my face, angry with the weather standing in our way of moving on, completely out of our control. It sounds petty when I put pen to paper, until I recall the emotional and physical exhaustion I'd already put my body through to get to this point, coupled with the antic-ipation that served as my drive to get through the tough and the scary parts, all the way to the summit. Whether in mountaineering or in another aspect of life, disappoint-ment outside of one's control feels like a massive punch in the gut. I knew that if we didn't move soon, my chances of summiting would be gone.

One night, I stayed behind after dinner and talked to the guide. "Look, I know there are other teams with the same company on the mountain," I said. "If we run out of time, am I able to go with another team?" Just as I had been on

Aconcagua, I was desperate to make it work and to do anything in my power to summit.

"We still have a couple more days until our up or down day," our guide reassured me. "Don't freak out just yet. We'll just see how it goes."

UP OR DOWN DAY

When up or down day came, we'd been on the mountain for fourteen days and hadn't even reached Denali's Base Camp. We needed to reach 14,000 Camp in order to have a chance at summiting, so we set out. The move was incredibly hard. Normally, we would have left gear buried in the snow halfway up so we didn't have to carry it all, but we were running out of days and didn't want to waste any more. There was one good day to move, so we did it—carrying our personal gear and the team gear, with one less person in the group. It was tough, but we made it.

By the time we got to 14,000 Camp, I had a throbbing headache. I was overheated and felt sick to my stomach. I wasn't strong enough to help set up our campsite. I put a baseball cap over my face to shield myself from the sun and I crawled into the first tent that had been setup, trying to rest and recover. My emotions were mixed: I was thrilled to be at a higher camp with great weather but struggled emotionally knowing that altitude always made me sick, just as it had on my four previous climbs. Knowing how my body reacted in the mountains, I knew I needed food, water, and rest in order to regain my strength. Luckily, the next day was a rest/skills day.

Above 14,000 feet, we would face steeper sections where we would have to clip our rope into anchors in the snow for protection. Anchors are metal pickets hammered into the snow with a carabiner attached to them. If anyone on the rope were to fall, the anchor would help catch them. Not everyone had used ropes/anchors in the past, so we practiced clipping in and out of the various anchors using carabiners. Our guide wanted us to be able to move quickly when ascending the higher part of the mountain, so getting familiar with the equipment was very important for those who weren't used to it.

The following day, we climbed to halfway between 14,000 Camp and High Camp at 17,200 feet, and we buried our cache—food, extra clothes, and other supplies. Afterwards, we climbed back down to 14,000 Camp. Out of all the days we had been on the mountain, this was my favorite: we didn't have to drag sleds anymore, and my pack was a manageable weight. We were finally doing technical climbing, going up fixed ropes and maneuvering steep ridgelines. These things are what fill my spirit when I climb; this is why I climb. We spent the night at 14,000 Camp and moved all the way to High Camp the next day, picking up our buried supplies along the way. From here, we knew we had the chance to summit Denali.

THE SUMMIT

On my past summit days, I had been told to take only what I thought I would need, making my pack as light as possible. My summit pack normally consisted of extra layers, snacks, and water. On Denali, though, the process was a bit different. We set off at 10:00 a.m. to summit, carrying our sleeping bags, sleeping mats, and other gear in case we got trapped and had to sleep on the mountain somewhere. I'd never carried a pack so heavy on a summit day.

Soon after leaving High Camp, we reached the Autobahn—an area I had been warned was the worst part of Denali. The Autobahn was a slick, steep ice hill we crossed by traveling sideways, digging our crampons into the ice beneath us as deeply as possible. My rope had three people: myself, the guide, and Red. If any of us were to fall, we would have to save each other; in this moment, we needed to function as one. This part of the climb was dangerous, and we had to focus on every single step. At one point, Red dropped his water bottle and we watched it fall for miles. As if we weren't already hyper-aware enough, here was an *extra* wake-up call.

After we made it across the Autobahn, we climbed higher until we eventually reached the Football Field—a large, flat area covered with snow about the size of a football field. With no elevation gain, this section was a perfect place to recover before the final push to the summit. I didn't have much of an appetite, but I forced myself to chew some grapefruit-flavored energy bites. Next came the final steep incline called Pig Hill. I'm not sure where it got its name, but what I do know is that it was hard. The air was thin, and I found it difficult to catch my breath. Every step was a challenge. We seemed to be going up at a very quick pace, and I was embarrassed to ask our guide to slow down but I knew I had to. I tried not to look up because the hill appeared endless. When we finally made it to the top, we took a short and much-needed break to fuel up for the summit ridge. I knew this was it: I had the fire inside of me to pull myself together and summit strong. The summit ridgeline was beautiful—a thin, not-too-steep snowy path on which we had to carefully pass a few fellow climbers who were on their way back down.

Finally, we were there: the summit of Denali. Yes, I was nothing short of thrilled to be there, but the climb wasn't over. My guide looked at me and said, "Liz, I thought you would be celebrating a bit more. This is five out of seven summits!"

"I never celebrate until I'm home hugging my family," I replied.

I was also aware that we still had to get down safely.

At the top, it was safe to unclip from the rope and explore. We took turns posing for photos with the different flags we had brought with us. The weather couldn't have been more perfect. There was no wind, and the sun illuminated the clear blue sky. I wore so much sun screen that my face was chalky white in all of the summit photos (a lesson learned from Kili, but no, it wasn't my most attractive look). While we waited for the other rope team from our group to arrive, we watched two men ski off the summit. I was envious, although the snow conditions for skiing were sub-par in my opinion.

THE DESCENT

The descent was long. My rope team made it back to High Camp right as the sun was setting, and the other rope team arrived in the dark because they were a couple of hours behind us. They were freezing and exhausted when they got to the tent.

The day after summiting, many teams opt to climb from High Camp all the way down to Base Camp because they want to get off the mountain—a trek often called the "death walk" or the "zombie march" because people are so exhausted by the time they reach the bottom. Because we had Sixty-Seven in our group, we stopped at 14,000

Camp for the night. While it was necessary to stop to ensure all members of the group could get down safely, I had to hand it to Sixty-Seven: he was one tough guy! I really admired his determination and I hope that at his age, I have the fitness and fortitude to do what he did. The next day, we traveled all the way down to Base Camp. At that point, I thought it was all downhill, but I was wrong. I had forgotten about a section called Heartbreak Hill.

At the beginning of the final day of our descent, I felt fine. I loaded my sled with most of my gear to keep my backpack light—a move perfect for downhill travel...*so I thought*. When we reached the flat part of the glacier, the temperature outside was unbearably hot. Because of the lack of slope and the power of the sun radiating off the sheer white, dragging our sleds was an arduous ordeal; instead of gently gliding them along a sheet of ice (as I had remembered), we had to pull them through slush. I was in an incredible amount of pain, facing the truest form of fatigue and exhaustion. Struggling to pull my over-packed sled, I began to crumble emotionally. This was the worst day of our climb.

Then we reached Heartbreak Hill, the last hill before Base Camp, where planes were waiting for us. Hauling my sled up that hill was what I imagine hell to be. It wasn't even steep, but mentally and physically I had had it. I was being pulled by the rope like a dog who hates his leash. I put one snowshoe in front of the other. I was done.

When we arrived at Base Camp, we discovered there were two seats left on the last plane of the day. My guide offered the seats to Red and me; the guide had to wait for the rest of the team that was still far behind us. Normally on my climbs, I like to do everything with my team, but Red agreed to board right away, and I followed suit. I was sick, I needed a toilet, and I felt downright miserable. I thought, *If I can sleep in a bed tonight, I'm flying, too.* I felt guilty, but it was simply one of those decisions I had to make. The plane was leaving, and I didn't have time to think.

BE PRESENT AND LET GO

Several times while on Denali, it didn't look like we were going to make it due to weather. The same is true in everyday life: things happen that are outside of your control, and they impact what you can and can't do. You have the choice to panic and break, or to accept the fact and push through using anything at your disposal.

When we were stuck for eleven days in that snowstorm, I spent so much time worrying about whether I would be able to summit, a situation that was completely out of my control. After the trip was over, I thought of all the opportunities to enjoy the beautiful Alaskan scenery that I had squandered because I was too concerned about what might or might not happen. Denali taught me to live in the moment, a skill that so many of us could practice on a daily basis.

Chapter 8

18,510 ft. (5,642 m) above Sea Level

The most beautiful thing you can wear is confidence.

—BLAKE LIVELY

Before leaving for Denali, I had booked another trip: Mount Elbrus in Russia. I planned it for three weeks after Denali, giving my body enough time to recover and hoping I would already be acclimatized altitude-wise. After spending twenty-one days reaching an altitude of 20,310 feet, depending on the person, the human body can remain adjusted to the altitude for an extended period of time. Planning Denali and Elbrus back-to-back, I was hoping to capitalize on my body's acclimatization, as well as my high fitness level. Not only was this the sixth summit on my journey to completion, but to me, this trip would be more than that. I was about to spend ten days with the jaw-dropping mountain guide I had seen walk into the Union Glacier tent in Antarctica; we can call him Mountain Man ("M" for short).

PREPARATION

After I connected with M about the Elbrus trip in January, we did much of our planning over email, meaning I still hadn't officially met him; I'd only seen him in Antarctica. When we finally met up in Seattle in March for coffee and to do more planning, I could feel my heart drop into my stomach. I drove from Vancouver to Seattle with some friends, and I was so nervous that my chest and neck broke out in hives. (Note to self: wear a turtleneck next time.)

I was incredibly attracted to him. I was infatuated, actually—one might say—*mildly* obsessed with him. I told my parents I wanted to marry him. Mild, right?

"Well, where are you going to live?" my mom asked. "Because he's always climbing different mountains all over the world."

"Mom, we're going to have kids and our kids are going to be children of the world!" I told her. "They're going to be running around Nepal with the Nepalese children." You may be thinking this is an exaggeration, but no, this was a real conversation, verbatim, even! Hold the judgment, please.

Even though I felt infatuated with M, I was realistic, too: his gorgeous eyes weren't all that had led me to choose him as my guide. I'd heard through his other clients that he was an exceptional leader on the mountain, with instincts you want guiding you every step of the way. Doing some more research, I was pleased to learn he was also a good skier. Believe it or not, not all mountain guides are good skiers. My ultimate goal was to summit Elbrus and snowboard down, so like I said, despite my infatuation, M was the perfect fit.

THE MOUNTAIN AND THE MAN

The highest mountain in Europe, Mount Elbrus is the

third lowest of the Seven Summits. Elbrus, Russia is a winter ski resort in the same vicinity as Sochi, where the 2014 Winter Olympics were held.

I didn't have a group this trip because I had M as a private guide. Some people in the mountaineering world use private guides when they climb as they prefer the comfort of having a guide who is familiar with their abilities and background, and who can give them undivided attention. Elbrus was my first privately guided trip, and I chose to hire M rather than join a company-led group because I didn't want other group members' skiing abilities to diminish my chances of snowboarding down, which was a very important part of my plans for this summit.

Our trip started off on the wrong foot, as M and I encountered an unforeseen logistical issue out of our control. Less than a week before we were scheduled to depart, M called to say his visa had been delayed. He had to fly to Houston to pick it up in person, so he was going to be a few days late meeting me in Russia. Cue the tears. I was heartbroken. His delay meant I was going to be in Moscow by myself, when all I really wanted was to be there with him, exploring a new city, finally getting a chance to get to know one another.

I flew to Moscow alone and kept myself busy by exploring the city. Moscow is a fascinating place with breathtaking architecture filled with rich history. Climbing the Seven Summits brought me to incredible parts of the world I wouldn't normally travel to, and for that I was always grateful. When M arrived, I was nervous but excited to see a familiar face after a few days of being on my own. From Moscow, we flew to a small town called Mineralnye Vody. From there, we hired a driver and took one of the wildest car rides of my life. The winding road felt like it would never end, and included speeding, swerving around animals, and flying over bumps. After a few hours, we finally arrived in a village called Terskol, where we spent the night in a little rustic hotel. Getting our bags up the four floors felt like climbing a mountain in and of itself. M would grab one end of the bag and I'd grab the other, and we'd slowly make our way up each of the staircases. I tried to breathe quietly so he couldn't tell I was winded from taking our bags to the top; I was *mortified*. Thank goodness M made a joke about that being part of our acclimatization process. Finally, I could breathe out loud again. The property was rather minimalist. There was not much beyond the basics, but my room was spacious, with a comfy bed, so I had nothing to complain about. Our time in Terskol was brief, but from what I saw, the town was simple, with a few gear rental shops and a handful of restaurants. We did a short day hike to help get acclimatized, and then it was time for Elbrus.

THE ASCENT

The climb up Elbrus starts over 12,000 feet above sea level. Instead of sleeping in tents, we stayed in huts the whole trip—it was straight out of a James Bond movie. The sleek, tube-like structures had bunk beds and modern decor. They also had Wi-Fi, and the chefs cooked us three meals a day in the dining hut. The view of the Caucasus mountain range was surreal. Two years ago, I had no idea I would be here, doing this, with *him*.

My other mountain climbs had involved moving between different camps along the journey, but Elbrus was different. Instead of going camp-to-camp, we stayed in the same place the entire time and climbed up and down on day hikes to make sure we were acclimatized before the summit push, which would last only one day.

M and I began to acclimatize the lower part of the mountain above the huts. It was straight up and down, nothing technical. On each acclimatization hike, M hiked up with his skis and I with my snowboard, and we skied and snowboarded down. It was fun, minus the part where I threw up the first day from the altitude. At least this mountain had beautiful bathrooms, so I didn't have to vomit in the snow—that was a plus.

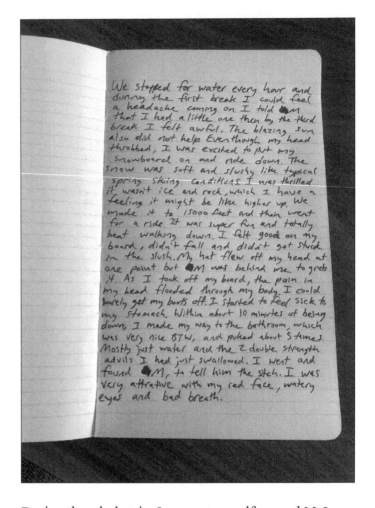

We stopped for water every hour and during the first break I could feel a headache coming on. I told M that I had a little one then by the third break I felt awful. The blazing sun also did not help. Even though my head throbbed, I was excited to put my snowboard on and ride down. The snow was soft and slushy like typical spring skiing conditions. I was thrilled it wasn't ice and rock, which I have a feeling it might be like higher up. We made it to 15000 feet and then went for a ride. It was super fun and totally beat walking down. I felt good on my board, didn't fall and didn't get stuck in the slush. My hat flew off my head at one point but M was behind me to grab it. As I took off my board, the pain in my head flooded through my body. I could barely get my boots off. I started to feel sick to my stomach. Within about 10 minutes of being down, I made my way to the bathroom, which was very nice BTW, and puked about 5 times. Mostly just water and the 2 double strength advils I had just swallowed. I went and found M, to tell him the sitch. I was very attractive with my red face, watery eyes and bad breath.

During the whole trip, I was not myself around M. I was shy, uncomfortable, and awkward; I could barely speak. No, really, I *didn't* speak. I'd thought that as the trip went on, I would become more comfortable, but I only grew more awkward. *PULL IT TOGETHER, LIZ!* M and I talked a bit, and our interactions were friendly enough, but I wasn't my normal self. Of course, I didn't have any true expectations of us, romantically. He was thirty-eight, and I was twenty-six; it was just a kindergarten crush. I knew M was extremely professional and that nothing would happen. This was his job, after all. I hadn't any time with M before the trip, so I didn't know much about him other than what I had gathered over phone and email. I was hoping he would be cocky and full of himself so that by the end of the trip, my perfect vision would be crushed and I would easily be over him. Of course, the world doesn't work like that. M was flawless.

THE SUMMIT

After five days of acclimatization climbs, our summit day had finally arrived. M and I woke at midnight and tried to eat breakfast, which was fruit, coffee, and a crepe, but we had eaten dinner not too long before, so neither of us was very hungry. We packed our gear into our packs eagerly and set off for the mountain. The day before, I had tested out carrying my snowboard boots in my backpack with all my other summit-day gear. The plan was for me to wear my mountaineering boots up the mountain and switch to my snowboarding boots for the descent. On summit day, the boots in my backpack were too cumbersome, so I decided to climb the whole mountain in my snowboard boots and crampons. I wasn't worried; I'd already tested that setup, and I knew I'd be fine.

We left at 2:00 a.m., walking into the pitch darkness with only our headlamps to guide us. When we got to 15,000 feet, M broke the news.

"I'm not comfortable skiing above here," he said, explaining his friend had tried a couple of weeks before and compared the experience to survival skiing—meaning conditions are icy, difficult, and dangerous. I was crushed. M said I could still bring my board and even offered to carry it for me, but I didn't want to snowboard down alone. I didn't think that was safe, and if he wasn't about to ski from higher than 15,000 feet, I didn't want to push it. He was my guide, and I knew he knew best; I needed to trust him, so I ditched my snowboard.

"I hope it's really sketchy at the top, so I don't feel bad for leaving my board," I said, upset.

During our earlier day hikes, we had never gone above 15,000 feet with our skis and board. But I think M had known before summit day that he wasn't going to ski from the top. After all, he had known the weather conditions. On the other hand, I'd never thought we *wouldn't* go all the way with our skis and board and descend as planned, and I wasn't thrilled.

When the sun came up on Elbrus that morning, the sky radiated a beautiful golden-orange glow that lit up the horizon as far as we could see, sitting just above the snow-grazed mountain tops. At 6:45 a.m.—four hours after we had left camp—we summited Mount Elbrus. There were several people on the mountain that day, but we were the first to reach the top. We had the summit all to ourselves, which is rare on popular mountains. After a few summit photos at the top of Europe, we began to make our way down the mountain.

After seeing the summit, I knew I was capable of snowboarding from it and that I should have brought my board to the top, but I didn't say anything. Because summiting

Elbrus is a one-day trip, I was tempted to ask if we could go back up the next day so I could bring my board, but I didn't want to push the topic. M had done his job—he had gotten me to the summit safely and would soon get me back down—so in the end, I let the topic rest.

On the way down, we saw a husky climbing with his owner, so I stopped to get some pictures with the dog. As a dog lover, this was a highlight. Then, we reached our skis and snowboard around 15,000 feet, put them on, and continued the rest of the way down.

After we'd completed the climb, we returned to Terskol. We tried to fly out a few days early, but we couldn't arrange it. Instead, we went horseback riding through the trees one day, and then fishing in a small pond another, before flying back to Moscow. We had our last dinner together, and then M and I parted ways. And just in case you were wondering, no, I never became less awkward. *Good one, Liz.*

My experience on Elbrus left me feeling somewhat disappointed—in myself, not in M or in "what could have been" a romantic relationship. Okay, yes, in my dream world, M and I had hit it off and had the best trip ever. Hey, a girl can dream!

Ultimately, I shouldn't have let my dream world cloud my real world, and I should have advocated for myself.

BE YOURSELF

If you can't even speak in front of someone, clearly, you might not be a good fit for "a future marriage and children of the world." I thought I was completely in love with M, but in actuality, I was infatuated with him. There's a difference. I couldn't speak up for myself around him, and I abandoned my goals because I didn't want him to think I was annoying or pushy when I asked for what I wanted. Moral of the story: don't abandon who you are as a person or what your goals are for anything—a job, a person, a role, etc.

LEARN TO HANDLE DISAPPOINTMENT

Could I have moped and been upset I didn't get the chance to snowboard from the summit of Elbrus? Could I have let sadness or disappointment over my lackluster interactions with M weigh me down long after I got back to my life in Canada? Yes, easily. Did I? Absolutely not. I recognize I made mistakes, and I learned from them—and no matter what the mistake is about, you can learn from them, too. No regrets. Ever.

P.S. M, if you ever read this, sorry you had to find out this way! :)

Chapter 9

7,310 ft. (2,228 m) above Sea Level

Do your little bit
of good where
you are; it is those
little bits of good
put together that
overwhelm the world.

—DESMOND TUTU

Regardless of the order I climbed the other six summits, I always knew I wanted Mount Kosciuszko in Australia to be my last one because I wanted my family and friends to be with me when I reached my final summit. At first, I thought it might be just my parents by my side, but I ended up having seventeen incredible people join me on the trip.

I knew climbing Kosciuszko would be the perfect way to end my Seven Summits journey, as the climb is an easy, one-day hike. I thought it would be a great mountain to celebrate on, but I wanted more than a celebration so I decided to turn my final climb into a fundraiser. Throughout several of my previous summit experiences, I'd heard stories of climbers using their climbs as a way to support a cause close to their heart. I wanted to do the same. I chose to fundraise for Canuck Place Children's Hospice in Vancouver. My family had been involved with the organization for about ten years, so it has been an important part of my life. Canuck Place is British Columbia's pediatric palliative care provider, offering kids with life-threatening illnesses, and their families, medical, emotional, and recreational support for as long as they may need, at no cost to the family. I never questioned this last climb would be for them.

Prior to the trip, I threw an event to help raise funds and awareness. I invited family and friends, did a Q&A, had raffle prizes, and showed a slideshow from my six previous climbs. I also had the opportunity to visit a children's camp that Canuck Place offers kids, giving them the chance to experience the joys and memories of camp life. While there, I sat with the kids and showed them bits and pieces of my climbs—gear, photos, stories. Afterwards, I asked them all to sign a flag that I would take with me to the top of Mount Kosciuszko. I wanted a way to take a piece of them with me. I also got the kids to write down a wish they had on special "flying wish paper." I told them I would bring their wishes with me and light them on the mountain. I would roll up each wish written on the paper, light them on fire and watch them fly beyond the clouds.

THE MOUNTAIN AND THE GROUP

The lowest of the Seven Summits, Mount Kosciuszko

is about halfway between Sydney and Melbourne. The Aussies call it "Mount Kozzy."

The seventeen people who joined me included my parents; some close friends from university, some of whom also brought their moms, which was really special; and some friends from high school who were living in Sydney and Melbourne at the time. My dad had lived in Australia when he was younger, so several of his friends still living in the area came out to join us. Honestly, I was a bit overwhelmed by how many people showed up. In that moment, I was able to truly visualize how much support I really had. Throughout my entire journey, on each of the previous summits, I had known it was the support and energy my loved ones gave me that helped me take one more step or one more deep breath. How lucky was I to climb the seven mountains that some people only dream of? The answer to that pales in comparison to how lucky I am to be loved and supported by these incredible souls.

Everyone wore matching T-shirts that I had made, displaying the Seven Summits in the order I had climbed them. I also made sure to download an app on my phone that enabled the children at Canuck Place to track my progress—and the progress of their flag—all the way to the top.

THE ASCENT

On the day of the climb, I woke up, got ready, and had breakfast. Many members of our group were trying to talk to me at once, and I began to feel overwhelmed. I left the breakfast table and went to my hotel room, where I burst into tears. I was so surprised by this sudden emotion that had welled up inside me. Despite the fact that Kozzy was the easiest of the seven, this was the biggest day of my entire life. Achieving this summit meant the end of my Seven Summit journey that had begun less than three years before. It meant that no matter what life put in front of me, I had the emotional, mental, and physical aptitude to overcome. No matter what your resume says, or what others believe, it's what you think of yourself that will allow you to succeed or fail. In those three years, I had met sides of myself I didn't know and experienced countless opportunities where my intuition, my mind, and my heart all needed to work in sync to make some of the most critical decisions I had ever faced. I knew that after I finished my Seven Summit journey, I would feel a sense of pride that no one, not even I, could ever erase. Although I was emotional, I pulled myself together and grounded myself in gratitude to have so many people supporting me.

We all met at the base of the mountain, excited to get going. Although there were a few other hikers on the trails, we were the only large group on the mountain. There was not a cloud in the sky, and I couldn't have dreamed up a better day for a hike, especially this hike. It was the only summit standing between me and the goal I had set for myself almost thirty-four months ago. Because many different trails lead up the mountain, we needed to check a map to determine the best route. The lower part of the mountain had some steep sections with built-in stairs supported by dirt and wood. Don't get me wrong, it was a solid workout, but you didn't lose your breath enough to prevent talking. Some people in the group chose not to hike the lower half, and they bypassed the initial section of the hike by taking a chair lift to roughly the halfway mark. From the point where the chair lift lets off, metal grates coat the ground, forming a beautiful path that leads all the way to the summit.

Overall, the climb up Kozzy was an easy walk, taking a total of six hours. I knew it was going to be anticlimactic; you don't need special equipment or any technical expertise. Nonetheless, the climb was satisfying. Along the way, I took turns talking with different people in our group. All of us were laughing and having fun the whole way up because it was a low-key trek, with everyone there to be a part of my journey and to have a mini-adventure for themselves. Even though there were eighteen of us creating a lifelong memory that morning, this summit wasn't just about us. I kept thinking about the kids from Canuck Place, and the looks and smiles on their faces when I told them about each of my climbs. I knew that as much as this hike was about marking the end of my journey, it was equally about honoring them. I decided to climb mountains for myself, to see how far I could push myself and how few comforts a human needs for the body to prevail and thrive in nature. However, this journey did not end up being about me. What put value in the journey is that it was bigger than I am, more important. I will always have the accolades associated with climbing these mountains. I realized the memories I created on each continent, on each ascent, and on each summit taught me invaluable lessons that only increase in value when they are shared. I started this for me, but now it's about everyone but me.

THE SUMMIT

The eighteen of us all summited together, but we weren't the only ones at the top; there were ten to twenty other people at the peak. We knew we had to get photos, so we made our way to the summit marker: a rock statue at the top. It was a bit of a war zone trying to get near it for a picture, and we needed to wait our turn for the quintessential summit shot. I required pictures for the media and Canuck Place, and the other seventeen hikers wanted various group photos, too. Reaching into my backpack to pull out the flag signed by the children, I was suddenly overwhelmed with emotion. In that moment, it was as if they were standing there with me, holding their flag in the wind, high above Australia.

In the midst of getting to the summit and taking photos, my friend's mom came up to me and gave me a hug. "Liz... Congratulations!" she said. "You completed the Seven Summits!" In that moment, it clicked for me: I had done it! From Kili to Kozzy, and every summit in between. We cracked open our Kosciuszko beers at the top and clinked our bottles in celebration.

We made it to the bottom as a group with smiles on our faces. I had mixed emotions. I was excited to have accomplished the goal I had worked so hard towards, but I was also sad that the Seven Summits were done. After some much-needed showers and decompressing, we regrouped for a massive celebratory meal at a rustic restaurant in the quaint mountain town where we were staying. A few people gave congratulatory speeches. Between every course, we rotated seats so we could all experience conversations and swap stories with different people in the group. I couldn't have dreamed up a better way to cap the Seven Summits. I was blessed to be surrounded by such supportive friends.

The best moment came when we realized we had raised over $213,000 for the children and families of Canuck Place. I couldn't have asked for a better way to wrap up my journey.

GIVE BACK

Summiting Kozzy was a reflective experience for me, as I had worked so hard for three years to complete the goal. But it was more than that. Although I grew up learning the importance of giving back, Kozzy taught me I truly could make a difference in the lives of others. Connecting my trip to this incredible cause—helping the brave children and families who have been dealt some of the most difficult hands life can offer—made the journey even more meaningful and reminded me that I was doing it for something other than myself. When you take the time to give back, it's often you who gets the greatest gift.

CHERISH YOUR SUPPORT SYSTEM

Kozzy was an easy hike, and it wouldn't have been much fun making the trek without family or friends. Sharing the experience with everyone made it incredibly special for me and helped me appreciate the value of a deep support system—a support system without which I wouldn't have made it through the toughest times throughout my entire journey and life.

Conclusion

All our dreams can come true—if we have the courage to pursue them.

—WALT DISNEY

LESSONS FROM MY SEVEN SUMMITS JOURNEY

- Try new things.

- Set goals, even if they feel big.

- Learn about and experience new cultures.

- Accept things beyond your control.

- Speak up and embrace opportunity.

- Believe in yourself.

- Keep the bigger goal in mind.

- Use—and actively seek out—positivity and motivation.

- Focus on connecting.

- Recognize the beauty around you.

- Be present and let go.

- Be yourself.

- Learn to handle disappointment.

- Give back.

- Cherish your support system.

Since completing the Seven Summits, my dad and I commemorated the experience by getting tattoos representing our climbs. I got an outline of all Seven Summits on my foot, and my dad got the outline of the two mountains he had climbed just above his ankle. On the day we got them done, my father went first, so there was no backing out for me. It was definitely a special bonding experience—and one I would have never expected to happen.

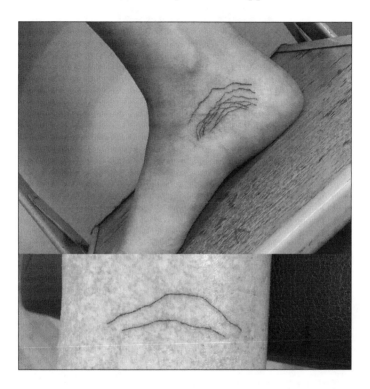

I have also pursued new adventures and accepted other challenges in my life. I'm currently a brand ambassador for PALU, a new outdoor apparel company specializing in technical cashmere for skiing and climbing, base layers, outerwear jackets, ski pants, and more. In the bigger picture, I know I want to keep climbing new peaks, setting new goals, exploring the world, and giving back as much as I can.

My goal with this book has been to show that while I climbed the Seven Summits, the lessons I took away from each adventure are applicable to so many other facets of life. It is the spirit with which we embrace the world that defines our success in the end. I hope my struggles and my achievements show you that no matter what you want to do and how challenging it may be to get there, all you need to do is say "yes." Once you agree to begin, you're already 90 percent closer to accomplishing your goal. Sometimes, you don't need to believe you can do it or be able to see yourself through the other end. All you need to do is remember who you *want* to be and how you *want* to live, and before you realize it, you've accomplished something that once seemed intangible.

My passion is the mountains, but yours doesn't have to be. Whether you want to run your first marathon, start your own business, or learn a new language, saying "yes" is the first step. Be compassionate with yourself and remember that you are the founder of your destiny. Finding your passion doesn't just benefit you, it will allow you to share a new sense of magic with the world.

To find out more about my journey and upcoming adventures, visit LizRoseSummits.com.

Appendix

EMAIL TO MY PARENTS AFTER I SUMMITED EVEREST

Omg hi parents! You guys should feel like
the happiest people in the world right
now, your wonderful twins turn 27 today
and you have the world's best mountain
climber as a daughter haha kidding but
omg it was so hard you legit have no
idea. Camp one to three was super hard
but doable and then life changed from
three to summit. I totally rocked it on
the way up the whole way though. First to
the summit, cheers to being 25 and not in
my mid forties. The oxygen was helpful
but it sure doesn't make you superman.

The lineup on summit night was worse than
Disneyland no joke just add -30 degree
weather. I knew it would be busy but it
was just a stand still of headlamps waiting
on a vertical hill. So crazy. Half way
to the summit my oxygen mask froze and I
couldn't breathe at all, my Sherpa checked
everything like the levels and pressure
and stuff and told me it should be fine
and then he figured out it was frozen
after me promising I couldn't breathe
a thing. So ya that was fun, poured

some hot water over a valve and it was fixed. I kept my cool because I knew we had three extra masks in case any broke. Oxygen bottles are so heavy omg my poor back, please book me ten massages.

The summit was legit tiny like smaller than our dining room table and some places were dangerous to be on. I got some photos but no way could you have had the photoshoot you dreamed of. During the trip there was so many times I wish I could have taken video and pictures but honestly it was way too hard. The videographer summited close to me and couldn't wait for Star at the top because we just had to get down asap. Going down was awful. I slipped with my crampons against a rocky part near the top and got super shaken up. I was attached to a rope so it was fine but just scary and I got super panicked thinking I legit had the rest of the mountain to get down. And first and second step were rock cliffs that were so sketchy, not to mention a massive dead body frozen in the middle of the two steps. I only saw one but some people saw two or three but like you could even see his poor frozen hands frozen flesh and all.

Anyways I pulled myself together and got down to camp three which is 8300 meters still super high but it was as far as we could get safely. And then the next day went from camp three to advanced base camp which we had insane wind and fog like so bad that's why not everyone made it down all the way but I couldn't go another day without telling you guys that I'm alive. It was so brutal. I knew summit day would be super long cold and hard but I didn't realize how many sketchy bits there would be. A guy in my group who has now done both sides said this side was way harder and way longer. Anyways I'm alive and all good.

Sorry to put you guys through the pain of waiting to hear from me. I am truly grateful for the accomplishment and the experience, but zero chance my kids are climbing Everest. I wouldn't even want a friend to go. It was truly that insane. The biggest summit is being down in one piece. I only have a few blisters and some sore spots on my face from my oxygen mask, sunglasses, and windburn. I am so lucky to be alive.

I love you guys soooooooo much!!! A June first night flight (like mine now is at 11pm or so or anytime on June second would be perfect).

I can't wait for the biggest hug in the whole world!!!! Xoxo

About the Author

Photo by Peter Lonergan

ELIZABETH (LIZ) ROSE is the youngest Canadian to conquer the Seven Summits. She accomplished this feat in under three years and is one of the few women in history to have done so. After receiving a communications degree from the University of Denver, Liz studied broadcast journalism at the New York Film Academy. Liz was raised in Vancouver, British Columbia, with older twin brothers. Liz attributes her adventurous spirit to the ocean and mountains at her doorstep. To learn more about her adventures, visit LizRoseSummits.com.

Manufactured by Amazon.ca
Bolton, ON

13668133R00116